DEVELOPING PUBLIC LIBRARY COLLECTIONS, POLICIES, AND PROCEDURES

A How-To-Do-It Manual for Small and Medium-Sized Public Libraries

KAY ANN CASSELL

ELIZABETH FUTAS

HOW-TO-DO-IT MANUALS
FOR LIBRARIES
Number 12

Series Editor: Bill Katz

NEAL-SCHUMAN PUBLISHERS, INC.
New York, London

Published by Neal-Schuman Publishers, Inc.
23 Leonard Street
New York, NY 10013

Printed and bound in the United States of America

Library of Congress Cataloging-in-Publication Data

Cassell, Kay Ann.
    Developing public library collections, policies, and procedures :
a how-to-do-it manual for small and medium-sized public libraries /
Kay Ann Cassell, Elizabeth Futas.
        p.   cm.—(How-to-do-it manuals for libraries ; no. 12)
    Includes bibliographical references (p.) and index.
    ISBN 1-55570-060-8
    1. Public libraries—Collection development—Handbooks, manuals,
etc. 2. Small libraries—Collection development—Handbooks,
manuals, etc. I. Futas, Elizabeth. II. Title. III. Series.
Z687.C38 1991
025.2′1874—dc20   91-9769
                                                                    CIP

CONTENTS

INTRODUCTION

This book is a manual designed to help those in small and medium-sized public libraries create collection development policies and, therefore, to better plan their collections. It consists of both the process used to develop a cohesive group of staff and community members to provide input into the collection development policy, no matter what the size of the institution, and the way to go about producing the collection development policy.

In recent years, collection development has become terribly important to the profession of librarianship and to the library's public. It is, to some, the most "professional" task that is done in the day-to-day work of the librarian. This is especially true of small and medium-sized libraries where the number of librarians is limited by the small portion of the budget allocated for staff. The staffing needs of an institution that is open to the public for a great many hours each week (often over 60 hours a week) are so great that the predominant use of its employees is to staff public service areas such as circulation and reference. Librarians, therefore, perform many different jobs, including administration, reference, cataloging, acquisitions, public relations, fundraising, budgeting, and the selection of materials.

The process of developing a collection in a library, surely one of the major tasks, is hampered by the need for the librarian(s) to devote a considerable amount of time to other tasks as well. In larger institutions, individuals may be able to specialize in collection development or even a particular subject area, but in smaller libraries, one person must often do many different jobs with little or no help.

In the world of libraries there are librarians who run libraries on their own, as the sole professional; those who guide a small staff of three or so librarians; and those who run a single or multibranch system with 10 to 25 librarians. These public libraries fall under the heading of small to medium-sized libraries. There are librarians who manage branches of large systems, and in other situations there are satellite or branch libraries staffed completely by support staff. Budgets of such libraries vary to a wide extent, from a low of about $25,000 to a high of close to $1,000,000. Some of these libraries do not consider themselves small, and yet still do not and cannot consider themselves in the same class as the larger libraries—either their budgets are small, their communities are small in population, or their resources are restricted in some other way. They could be considered, for the sake of this manual, medium-sized public libraries. It is for these professionals and their hard-working staffs, who find themselves in any of the above situations that this volume is written.

The process of collection development should consist of:

- learning the goals, objectives, and priorities of the institution;
- learning about the collection that currently exists and the relationship it bears to the community it serves;
- developing a policy to select, acquire, discard, maintain, and evaluate collections from this time forward;
- learning how and what to select and acquire for the clientele you now have;
- learning to recognize what needs to be looked at and how frequently, to make sure that your client base has not changed in the years since you last looked at it;
- developing procedures to handle the policies that were designed;
- developing procedures to evaluate, revise, and pass on these policies to future patrons, board members, staff, and librarians who join after the process has been completed.

All of these activities take time and effort on the part of the individuals interested in going through this process to mold a collection development plan. *Developing Public Library Collections, Policies, and Procedures* will help you to recognize who the people in your community may be who will want to serve on the collection development committee, how to organize them so that they function well, what goes into the collection development document, what other documents are needed so that a "plan" really exists, and how to assure, when documents are finished, that the plan continues to flourish. It is too easy to end prematurely, once the process has reached the goal of producing a policy statement. Some libraries just write the document, publish it in some form (sometimes photocopying it for just the staff and sometimes producing a glossy broadside or pamphlet for patron consumption), and decide that they are at the end of the process, when they are barely in the middle. Chapter one consists of a discussion of the purposes of collection development along with some definitions, who should be involved, and when that involvement should take place. The setting of the stage for the beginning of the process is introduced. Chapter two discusses how to set up the process by which the collection plan will begin. It consists of a detailed account of how to set up a group, who should be in the group and why, what roles certain individuals should play, and how the process should be managed and by whom. Chapter three concerns the gathering of information about the library and evaluating its collections. Trying to determine what is known about the library's collections is an important first step in determining what the collection should look like. In this chapter current policies of the library (e.g., circulation, staffing, reference, etc.) are explored, and their impact on collections is discussed. Chapter four describes community analysis. How to collect information on the community and what that information can mean to a collection development plan. Chapter five describes a collection development policy statement for a small public library. Chapter six summarizes the steps in the process. It stresses the importance of an ongoing process to meet new demands and to include new patrons in future collection decisions. This allows flexibility to meet new demands and to include new patrons in future decision making. The appendixes include a sample collection development policy, and a bibliography which points to further information on both the designing of the process and the writing of the policy statements. This manual will show practicing professionals how to evaluate and to continue to develop a collection suitable and valuable to their institutions and the communities that they serve.

 # SETTING THE STAGE

This chapter will guide the librarian through the process of formulating a collection development plan. This, in turn, will lead to more effective and efficient collection development since policy statements act as blueprints for action. Although the policy itself is important in the development of a library's collection, the process we go through in creating the policy is just as important. We need to understand the background within which the decisions affecting the building of collections have been made and thus how this policy has evolved.

It is easy to write a collection development policy in the abstract, but the policy then may be erroneously based on little knowledge and understanding of the community and of the library as it is at present. To be effective the policy must grow out of its environment. This fundamental tenet for collection development policies and procedures cannot be overemphasized. Book costs continue to rise, and most libraries do not have unlimited budgets, so careful decision making is extremely important. Newer formats are being introduced into the collections of even the smallest of public libraries. These formats appear, on the surface, to be much more expensive than traditional print formats. Libraries must make decisions not only about books but about recordings, tapes, CDs, films, video, and even computer software. Careful decision making in all phases of collection building becomes more and more important as the number and complexity of the formats grow.

THE PURPOSE OF PLANNING

Libraries, as institutions, are fairly complicated in both structure and function. They have a complex arrangement of space, uncommon organization of materials (at least to those not in the field), and numerous personnel who conduct business differently from those in other institutions (as one example, in what other institution does personnel spend most of the time putting stock back because clients are allowed to wander around taking anything they want from the shelves).

Whenever there is a large expenditure of public monies, it is best to have a guide to planning where and how it all fits together. Thus, when the taxpayer needs an accounting of money spent, the institution will be able to provide it since its budgeting procedures also derive from its policies. The collection development plan is like a business plan for a small business. Such a plan is devised to guide the development of your "business." One could say it is a road map which outlines the steps to be taken to accomplish the goals of the business.

In the case of the "library business," the plan will define the market, describe the product(s) and the services to be provided, and present a budget in order to project the costs to accomplish the goals of the plan. That is why you need to know all you can about the community you serve. Just as in a small business, you must know your market before you can even attempt to sell the product. To be successful requires not only identifying the market (knowing the community) but describing the product (the materials that are available and how to acquire them) and the services, publicizing the service (your library, its materials, its programs, etc.), and accounting for the money (in this case, since the profit motive is not present, this might mean accounting for public dollars spent). For everything there is a reason, and collection development planning is no exception.

The purpose of the collection development plan in the library setting is:

1. To establish guidelines for the present and future staff to develop the collection.

    These guidelines will outline the techniques to use to select materials on a day-to-day basis by subject, level, type, and format. The plan should allow for the development of guidelines for collection maintenance as well, (weeding, evaluation, inventory, etc.), and for policy formation.

2. To formulate guidelines for in-service training of current and future staff.

    The collection development process should extract values and ethics from the group that devises it and create a written document (the policy) to pass down this information to the next generation without them having to go through all of the planning again. Through the guidelines set forth, new staff would get a clear picture of the institution's philosophy, mission, goals and objectives, and policies. The staff can then maintain uniformity in the design and the development of the collection.

3. To provide a tool for decision making in the area of

budgeting for the physical plant, the personnel, and the materials by describing the process to use.

With an intelligent and tailor-made policy designed and produced by the people most familiar with and interested in the institution, by a process which itself creates within the group dynamic a spirit of belonging and a sense of community, the end product will benefit from the group process. It will help those involved to prepare a coherent, long-range financial, management, and personnel document, which will make planning easier in the future in all areas.

4. To clarify the relationships among the board of trustees, the library staff, and the community and to establish their respective responsibilities.

The process of planning can ensure a higher level of understanding among these groups and define how each member can contribute to collection development without impinging on the rights, authority, and responsibilities of the others.

5. To allow staff to become accustomed to the task of responding to questions about materials collected and to provide a well-thought-out statement should they need to defend the library against censorship and other considerations of a personal nature.

The plan will create a product, the collection development policy, which will serve as one of the library's primary documents that explains to the public why certain materials are in the collection. If a particular item in the library's collection is challenged, the board of trustees will have a written document explaining the rationale for it having been selected for the collection. The document may list the criteria for adding materials, maintaining a certain level of development in an area, and the procedures used in making selections. In developing such a document, the group process assures that there will be a detailed explanation of these and other decisions. If the explanation is not in the written document, then it will be in the minutes of meetings held to decide on the policy document that led to the creation of the collection development policy.

THE PROCESS OF PLANNING

TO BE SUCCESSFUL:

To be successful:

- identify the market
- describe the product and the service
- publicize the service
- account for the money spent

We start with the process. It leads to the product, which is a collection development policy. The process is, for many reasons, the most important part. The surveying, studying, and discussing of areas to be part of the final product is what makes the collection development planning process so valuable and the policy which follows a viable and useful document. It is not something written by a group relying on its own best instincts and knowledge. But rather it is a product of a group representing different aspects of the library and its community.

Through this process of meeting, researching, analyzing data, and evaluating ideas, the final product will represent a broader mix of interests and concerns and be more inclusive of all participants' ideas on the subject of the collection and, therefore, a more meaningful and useful document to the library and its public. It also will be a document, depending on how the planning process is conducted, which has as its underpinnings the support of a diverse group of citizens and library staff. These groups understand why certain decisions were made and are prepared to talk about how they arrived at this document and publicize it to the community.

One of the most important parts of the process of developing a collection and writing a collection development policy statement is to involve as many people as possible in order to get a cross-section of ideas from the library and the community. These groups of people may see things that a single individual with a single focus might miss; in addition, by being part of the process of development of the collection policy, they may take an added interest in the entire process. This may reap benefits in the future when putting into effect the decisions of the group to accomplish the goals of the library and its community.

In the case of large city, county, or multibranch system libraries, many of the people that the planning process will draw upon are librarians who can work on their own, with a common language and a common background, to produce a cogent document about the collection they are building. In the case of a small institution, this is not possible. But here, the impossibility of having many librarians in the process may, in fact, turn out to be a benefit in the long run. Involving others such as the support staff, trustees, Friends, and patrons will broaden the scope of the document. It will enable the librarians on the committee to really talk to the other committee members, instead of always to themselves, and will help to create a vocal, concerned, and active support group for the library and its collections.

If it appears that the process of developing this plan is taking too long, costing too much, or creating more problems than it is solving, think again. If the first steps, i.e., setting up the initial process under which the plan will be created, is not done with a certain amount of care, the entire process—including the policy document and the collection created as a result—may be useless. The process is important because it sets the stage not only for the document but for all of the collection building that comes after the document is developed. If the process is abandoned too early in favor of some product, it will be difficult to pick up where it left off. (For example, a public library that does not have a primary process committee which is representative of the community may find segments of the community have been left out of the product, the policy, and then left out of the library!) Then the process must begin all over again, a time-consuming and often not a very feasible solution.

It is equally important to be careful at the time of the creation of the policy document. It is hard not to think of the policy statement as the end of the process, but it is not. For example, once a public library has developed its collection development policy, it is a temptation just to file it away. This can happen even before the board of trustees has reviewed the results and had a chance to approve the policy. If this is allowed to happen, it becomes a policy only of the library and represents just those who worked on it from the library. In truth it must be understood and accepted by a much larger audience. It must be understood by the board, the Friends' group, the staff, and the patrons, as well as those in the community who do not use the library but who may know about it or vote on its budget.

What is actually in the document will depend on what its aims are and for whom it is written or developed. There are many possible groups for whom the document might have been developed, among them are the library's users, its staff, its board, and the professional community in the area of which they are a part.

For whomever the document is written, bear in mind at all times that the document is just one step on the way to collection development. It is a blueprint for accomplishing something, not the accomplishment itself. Do not mistake the policy for the process of collection development. The process, to paraphrase McLuhan, is the message; the product is the medium by which that message is translated to its public, whether that public is the staff, the librarians, the patrons, the board, or the professional community.

WHO NEEDS A COLLECTION DEVELOPMENT PLAN?

Everyone who is connected with the library should understand the need for a plan in building a library collection. The plan consists of a collection development document that demonstrates in black-and-white the composition of the collection, documents how and why it was built up the way it was, and serves as a guide for librarians who are selecting materials for the collection. It may also consist of various procedures that libraries create to help in the organization and ongoing activity of building a collection for the community. Some of these procedures can protect the community and the institution of the library, as well as those who work in that institution, from censors. Others may outline how to do an inventory, how to collect various statistics for decision making, and how to do a community analysis. These procedures will be discussed in later chapters.

THE POLICY

The collection development document can be a public relations tool for the library to use with its various publics: its board, Friends, volunteers, staff, community, patrons, and the government of the municipality in which the library operates. It also ensures continuity during changes of staff and board personnel and is valuable to new community members. Since it is written, it will be there to justify, to explain, and to teach coming generations of patrons and staff about what went into building the services and materials in the library.

The policy is also beneficial to those who were involved in the conception and production of the plan and who wish to have their memories jarred or their decisions backed up by historical precedent. Historical precedent may be valuable at times of stress and strain—either budgetary or philosophical.

Libraries often have a general collection development policy and make their selections based on a set of guidelines passed on by word of mouth. In some cases they have revised the unwritten guidelines to fit what they think the library needs. Such an informal approach can be dangerous and can lead to misunderstandings on the part of other library staff, the board, and the community. The process of writing a collection development policy makes the library examine what its unwritten and written procedures are.

TIME

What is needed is the time:

—to select members for the committee who will help to formulate the collection development plan,
—time for the committee to meet,
—time for research to be done, and
—time for information to be generated from surveys, questionnaires, and interviews.

This process of examination is important, because it provides an opportunity to ask questions and obtain more points of view.

THE PROCEDURES

The way in which a library gets things done, its procedures, can be embedded in a document, such as the collection development policy or in a manual of its own. In many libraries, procedures are orally presented to newcomers, usually at the worst possible time (after a crisis) or right before the commencement of a long, involved, procedural imperative (such as an inventory). Whatever the decision about where to include procedures, the process by which they are discussed, analyzed, and promulgated will in itself be a time of learning for most of the individuals on the process committees.

WHO SHOULD BE INVOLVED—AND WHEN

The process of collection planning and the writing of the collection development policy and procedures should involve everyone from the librarians, support staff, Friends, board members, and patrons, to the community leaders, and volunteer workers. All of those who are interested in the library as a cultural institution in the town or city should be interested in helping to develop the collection; all who are interested should get involved. That is the widest net to spread when asking for members to help achieve this plan. What you will wind up with will be those with special interests, time to spare, and those who want to become involved in the community in some way. A call should go out as soon as the librarian decides that the collection has become a priority. This should attract enough people to help reach out to other areas of the community and ask for more help. Eventually a sizable group should be encouraged to come to an open meeting. The librarian should set out the agenda and indicate how involvement will take place, the amount of time that will be needed, and the reason community involvement is necessary. Stress what can be accomplished, The group that coalesces after that first meeting will be the core of the collection development planning group. Among the items that must be prepared for a nonprofessional group are definitions of what is meant by the terms we so casually use in referring to our collection of materials. Among the terms needing to be defined are:

Collection Development: The process of setting up ways in which the library can make decisions on what materials to spend its money on. This includes knowing what is being published now and in the near future, what material is presently in the library, what material should be in the library, and a design for getting the library's collections to better represent the latter ideal.

Collection Building: The art of choosing the best material for a specific group of people, in a specific location, at a specific time.

Collection Management: Making decisions based on knowledge of the process of collection development while taking into account the art of collection building to produce meaningful collections for the community and the institution served.

While trying to build a collection, there are certain factors that enter into any decisions that are made. These affect the ability of the librarian to obtain the best material that is being published, no matter what format, language, or place of publication. Among those factors are cost (or budget); staff (to select, purchase, catalog, disseminate, weed); space (the area available to house the purchased material); availability (determining if items are available through jobbers or from publishers, or if the library can afford to go to a used or rare book dealer to locate them); and time (the amount of time needed to locate items or to process them for use, e.g., for a paperback that must be hardbound to make it last longer, or for a volume containing a diskette in a pocket, which must be handled differently from an ordinary volume, or for time to weed a section of the collection).

Collection Evaluation: The use of scientifically based statistics to determine the value, both past and present, of a collection of materials from a particular library and what the value is to a specific group of patrons. Finally, generalizations which might be made from the results of such an analysis to other libraries with similar characteristics.

Collection Use: A term used to denote studies done in particular libraries that measure the circulation of materials and then, based on these statistics, generalize on the value of the entire collection. Most large libraries have done such studies of their collections, and the literature abounds with reports on these studies. In recent years, criticisms of the earlier literature has prompted a more sophisticated methodology to study use: An inquiry is made into noncirculating collections, in-house use, and what is meant by "use," if it is not clear whether the material was literally used or useful to the patron.

With the definitions and purposes in place, the next step in creation of a collection development plan tailored to your library is to create the group that will develop the plan.

2 HOW TO CREATE A PROCESS

At the start of the collection development plan is the process from which everything else flows. At the very beginning, it is best not to worry about the desired product but to concentrate on creating a process. This, in turn, will allow for an atmosphere in which plans can be formulated and decisions can be made. Since a process always takes a great deal of time and effort, it is fair to say that time is the biggest commitment to be made.

What is needed is the time to select members of the committee who will help to formulate the collection development policy, time for the committee to meet, time for research to be done, and time for information to be generated from the surveys, questionnaires, and interviews. Where does all of this time come from? Time has to be allocated for this process from an already busy schedule. In fact, since full-time staff will be participating in a highly visible way, the library director and board members must be willing to have this involvement take place during work hours or to compensate them if it involves night or weekend meetings. The staff must feel and see the library's commitment to the creation of a well-thought-out and well-developed collection plan. Only with the institution and the institution's top administrators and trustees behind it can you expect any level of commitment from the staff.

As a first step in the process, the pre-planning meeting must take place with the library director, the board, and other designated, interested parties who should sit down to prepare a budget. Funds will need to be appropriated for a variety of expenses. Money will be needed to hire consultants and part-time staff to relieve those working on the plan of some of their regular duties, as well as to buy those materials identified as necessary to fill the gaps discovered during the process. It might be possible to get a grant from a local or regional government agency, but it is more likely that you will have to plan at least a year in advance to get these expenses into line items in your budget.

Once the money has been earmarked for the process, and the time set aside in a general sort of way, the next activity is to choose or identify people to serve on the committee. Since board support is crucial to the process, members must understand in some detail how the process will work. They should be apprised of the timeline, the energy, and the materials committed by the library and staff. Have at least one board member involved so he or she can share information with the rest of the board. Provide frequent reports on the planning process so members will understand what is going on and can answer questions asked by community residents. In addition to the librarian and the board, other members of the process committee can be representatives from any number of

The process of collection planning and the writing of the collection development policy and procedures should involve everyone from the librarians, support staff, Friends, board members, and patrons, to the community leaders and volunteer workers.

15

groups, organizations, or the general public. The process depends on the successful interaction of these people when they come together, their cohesiveness as a group, and their commitment to the idea of the collection development plan.

STRUCTURING THE PROCESS

It is important to have some idea of how to go about the process of planning—and to follow it—because people have a tendency to hurry certain of the more boring or less exciting elements of the process or to skip them altogether. It may take a full meeting of the board and staff to decide who should be planning committee members and how they should be approached about joining the process. All members of the board and library staff should be consulted about who should be included in these plans. Take the time to ask for contributions from everyone who has the interest and patience to see the process to its conclusion. Spend some time explaining what the process will be as the group chooses members. When it appears that interest is flagging, stop the process for some good, old-fashioned pep talks. If you follow these suggestions, then those parts of the process that are least exciting, but still important, will be completed, the right people chosen for the committee, and the group will have a better chance to create a successful product. If the committee becomes unwieldy as you structure the process, you may want to break it up into subgroups and assign each a task. Possible subgroups might include:

- Goals and Objectives,
- Community Analysis,
- Community Resources,
- Criteria for Selection,
- New Technology,
- Networking and Consortium Commitments,
- Specialized Clientele, and
- School and Library Relations.

Each of these subgroups adds information of interest to the plan and contributes to the process through information collected or ideas formulated. This list points up how important choosing committee members is. Whether there are subcommittees or these tasks are accomplished by the committee as a whole, all of these tasks must be done, so the right people are needed for the process. A great deal of discussion goes into this work. One person cannot hope to have all of the ideas and the time needed to present all the information to the group. Figure 2-1 outlines the roles of the participants in the process.

CHOOSING COMMITTEE MEMBERS

AT LEAST ONE MEMBER OF THE COMMITTEE SHOULD:
—know the community,
—have a background in community history,
—have expertise in creating and producing surveys.

ALL COMMITTEE MEMBERS SHOULD:
—like to work and get things done,
—know the library,
—have time to participate,
—be able to work well with others.

There are many facets to the collection development planning process, so you will need many people with many different skills and ideas. Represented in this group should be those who:

* know the community, perhaps even leaders or "gatekeepers" within the community itself;
* have historical background;
* have knowledge of changes manifested in the last decade or so;
* have expertise in creating and producing surveys of useful questions for the public to answer; and
* like to work and get things done, perhaps some of the most tireless volunteer workers that your community has produced.

The success of the project rests on your ability to solicit a wide spectrum of involvement—staff, board, volunteers, Friends, patrons. Each of these groups has a valuable role to play in the eventual success of the process and in the final product: a policy that truly reflects the community to be served.

Figure out the minimum number of people needed to accomplish each of these activities. Then add some others who will determine the current state-of-affairs in the library itself. These could be from the staff and others who know the library itself very well. Then double that number to determine how many people should be on the committee. Committee members should have:

* knowledge of the library's services and collection,
* time to participate in the process,
* ability to work well with others,
* some specific knowledge and/or skills as mentioned above,
* ties to larger groups within the community organization or town government.

FIGURE 2-1 ROLES OF PARTICIPANTS IN THE PROCESS

WHAT	WHO
Planning the process	Director/Board
Budgeting money and time	Director/Librarians
Outlining procedures	Director
Creating the committee	Director
Choosing members for committee	Entire staff
Running committee meetings	Director (or other designated member)
Developing subcommittees to handle tasks	Entire committee
Choosing people to manage subcommittees	Entire committee
Assigning tasks within subcommittees	Heads of subcommittees
Developing timetables	Members of subcommittees
Keeping subcommittees on track	Heads of subcommittees
Holding meetings of various subcommittees	Heads of subcommittees
Reporting on results of tasks done by subcommittees	Heads of subcommittees

You should choose people who will not quit when the going gets rough, because there may be times when everything is not calm and well-organized. During the process it will be useful to provide some kind of members' recognition and encouragement. For example, one library holds an annual reception to which the press is invited and during which they honor their staff, the Friends' group, and volunteers with service pins, certificates, and plaques for the special effort that they have put into the library and its functioning in the past year. This could be extended to include the collection development planning committee, as well. Another library holds an occasional lunch or reception to celebrate achieving a specific goal or objective.

LEVELS OF INVOLVEMENT

The staff, both librarians and support staff, should be drawn upon for all the processes that revolve around collection building. Let us look at several groups and individuals, summarized in Figure 2-2, to see where their involvement would be most useful.

THE DIRECTOR

The director's contribution is one of coordination rather than advocacy of any one point of view. The director sees the need for collection development and begins implementation. The director is the one, perhaps in conjunction with the board, who chooses the players.

Since there are often few librarians in small libraries, it may not be possible to disengage the director from direct involvement with the collection development process. In these libraries the director of the library is almost certainly the leader of the group's deliberations. If this is your situation, the director must do everything possible to maintain objectivity and avoid exerting too much influence. The director can lead a group and still maintain impartiality.

The leader of a group, according to most parliamentary rules, does not vote except in the case of a tie. The leader usually does not speak to the question on the floor either, except in unusual circumstances. To that end, the director as group process leader takes the role of facilitator, not as director of the library, and maintains that position throughout the entire process. As with most facilitators, this one should start meetings and run them:

FIGURE 2-2 LEVELS OF COMMITTEE INVOLVEMENT

WHO	WHAT	WHEN
Director	Leads entire function	From beginning and throughout
Librarians	Lead subcommittees, may lead committee in place	After commitment to commence project
Support Staff	Subcommittee members	From inception of subcommittees
Board of Trustees	Knowledge of entire project, may be members of committee or subcommittee	From beginning and throughout
Volunteers	Subcommittee members	From inception of subcommittees
Friends	Committee members of subcommittee members	From start of committee process
Patrons	Committee members or subcommittee members	From start of committee process

draw up the agenda, see that the group sticks to the agenda, and accomplishes any tasks either during the meeting or those assigned between meetings. Among the tasks that need to be performed between meetings are the distributing of questionnaires, conducting interviews, gathering information, taking inventories, etc. It is up to the facilitator to see that these are done on time and reported to the group so that the entire group has the same information upon which to make decisions as they arise.

LIBRARIANS
If you have several librarians on the staff, involve them all. Those librarians who deal directly with building a library's collection should be the most heavily involved, but do not ignore the cataloger and the circulation librarian—a librarian from another area can make significant contributions to the process exactly because he or she brings another point of view.

As with other members of the committee, it is important to have a firm commitment from the professional staff. You will be asking them to chair and serve on subcommittees such as goals and objectives, mission of the institution, resources inside and outside the library, etc., and to do a great deal of the background research. They must feel the importance of the desired product so that they can be completely committed to the process.

It is extremely important to have some professional staff on the committee. If your library is so small that you are the only professional, look for librarians who live in the community but either work in neighboring towns or are retired librarians and are part of some other group (i.e., Friends, volunteers, or even the board). You might also consider using librarians from other kinds of libraries in your area. The importance of librarians to the collection development committee in both the planning and implementation stage cannot be overemphasized.

SUPPORT STAFF
Support staff that spends its working day with the public, behind the scenes with the library materials, or in adjunct positions to service points often have good perceptions about what is going on in their areas and throughout the library. You may have an enthusiastic staff member who knows all the patrons by name—or by reading interest. Or you may have a support staff person who really wants to be a part of things that happen and has the dedication and the ability to carry projects through once started. These are the people, no matter what status they hold in the library, who make good team members.

For example, circulation staff could be placed on the subcommittee creating and carrying out the in-house survey since they know the best time of day, day of the month, and time of year to survey patrons so that the widest possible group will be reached (for an example of an in-house survey, see chapter four). For instance, in one library, due dates are the same day of the week no matter what day they are checked out. Because the circulation staff knows that two large patron groups—senior citizens and parents with young children—never come in on that day because of the crowds, they make sure that the in-house survey is not taken exclusively on a due date but is sometimes conducted on another day of the week in order to get the seniors and nonworking parent's opinions on issues.

Another good example of staff expertise is knowledge of the community. Often the staff of the library, by dint of its job in service areas, gets to know a great deal about what is going on in the community. When looking for information, whether historical or current, about what is available and who is knowledgeable about the community, support staff may be a wonderful resource. Many people in service positions are happy in their work because they are curious about people and have a knack for making friends. You will sometimes find this among bank tellers, store clerks, and even among the police and fire fighters. A lot of public service work is done by these groups who meet local people, at ordinary and usual times in their lives, strike up conversations, and learn things about them. People with this kind of personality can be vital to a project that needs to collect useful information on the community and its informational and recreational needs. Support staff is an extremely valuable addition to the collection development planning process. Use the staff interest form (Figure 2-3) to gather information.

BOARD OF TRUSTEES

It is proper, cost-effective, and realistic to bring in whoever is going to be important at the end of the process, at the beginning. Involving trustees at the beginning means that later they will be capable of explaining the process and why certain decisions were made as opposed to others. This turns into both a cost saving in time and helps you to have an ally on the board when money is allocated for the project. Select board representatives with great care, since it takes a special kind of person to act as liaison to the rest of the group without seeming to take over the prerogatives of the board. What is needed in this instance is a person who does not

FIGURE 2-3 STAFF INTEREST FORM

1. Are you interested in being part of the collection
    development process? _____yes _____no

2. Please indicate which of the activities listed below you
    would be interested in participating in:

    _____ Community Analysis

    _____ Community Resources

    _____ Questionnaire Development

    _____ Goals and Objectives Statements

    _____ Weeding Criteria

    _____ Selection Criteria

    _____ Evaluation Planning

    _____ Writing

    If you are interested in more than one, please indicate your
    order of preference with #1 being the area of greatest interest,
    #2 second, etc.

3. Do you have any hobbies, or outside interests that might be
    important in developing collections in subject or fiction
    areas? (For example: mysteries, romance, westerns, auto
    repair, household repairs, cooking, decorating, etc.)

    _____
    _____
    _____

4. Is there anything not listed on this form that you think
    might be interesting to the Library? Be specific.

    _____
    _____
    _____

    Thanks.   Please return to the Director's Office.

offend anyone, who presents issues in an unbiased manner, and who is generally liked or respected by the other members of the board.

If a member of the board of trustees is willing to become part of the entire process, it is to your advantage. If you have this opportunity, it will help when the time comes to ask the board as a whole for approval. Then you will have someone to interpret those parts which might cause conflict or which are difficult to understand. For example, the collection development committee of a library decided to include strong wording on the privacy of information in the policy statement, which it knew would be controversial. Rather than have the librarian present the issue to the board, the committee members decided to have a committee member who was also a board member present it, since she had always avoided conflicts with other board members and was respected by them all. Since the committee member supported the policy and was also the board representative, the board accepted the recommendation to adopt the policy statement.

There are parts of the process of developing a collection in a library for which board members are particularly well suited. Since they represent a group of established leaders almost by virtue of the position they hold, they know a lot about the people who make up the community, even if those people never use the library. Board members can reach out to the community through their constituencies and help promote the interests of the library in the community.

If the collection development process is not led by the director or a librarian, then a logical person to take charge is someone on the board. A public librarian who has a good rapport with the board can easily depend on board members to carry out the process on the highest level. The board always expects to be involved on the highest level, and this is most appropriate for them.

You will need someone who, by virtue of his or her past experiences, will command the respect of everyone else in the group. A board member may have had other positions of authority in which he or she learned how to conduct the group process or run effective meetings. Any person skilled in the facilitator role is a good choice to lead; but if no one is skilled, then the best person for the job is someone who is respected and who handles authority well.

The board of trustees can make an enormous contribution to the process of building a collection to fit the community it serves. By its very nature, it represents the community and provides one part of the library's public relations. Board members are often active in other groups and can represent the library at appropriate meetings.

Their participation in the library's activities and in the development of a collection may be the key to its success.

VOLUNTEERS

Many public libraries with a regular corps of volunteers may want to invite them to participate in the process. It will be interesting for them to serve on the collection development committee; no doubt they will have insights to offer. There are two things to be sure of before inviting members of this group to participate: be sure that they want to attend and try to choose only those who like to accomplish tasks. They, like the others from the board or Friends' groups, are often overcommitted and overextended in time. Do not abuse them for the sake of the process. They are an important part of your community and you will want them to remain so, long after the process has produced a plan and, from that, a policy.

FRIENDS

The members of Friends' groups always like to be asked to help. These people usually are heavy users of the collections. Therefore, they bring a patron's values and interests to the process, as well as knowledge of the library from their Friends' activities. The best person to pick from a Friends' group is one who is enthusiastic about the library, the collection in general, and about the process of developing guidelines for collection building and evaluation in the future. Include those people who would like to be included. They are particularly valuable in a community analysis. Members of a Friends' group may know a lot more about the town or city than you, since they are often life-long residents or long-term employees of the community and active in other organizations. The Friends' group as a whole might also be asked to take on some specific part of the process, for example, in-house or community survey, if you choose to do one.

PATRONS

Another group to include in the process is the patrons. Young adult users tend to be an invisible part of the library's user population, but a bright and eager high school student might be a valuable addition to the process group. A student aide or a student getting a library degree might be interested in outside activities geared toward their career choices. For a view of the half of the population, which often uses the collection the most, look to the younger patrons for advice. Remember, those fifth graders that we all read about after they have become writers, teachers, or lawyers—who were "saved by the library"—might be enticed into getting involved in the process of collection development.

Adult patrons may be interested in getting involved, as well. In one library, for example, there was a researcher who used the library regularly and was interested in the library's collection. Because he had a flexible schedule, he became a committee member. Post a sign to draw in this kind of person. If you or your staff know of such a person, invite him or her to join the group.

LEADERSHIP

A leader should be chosen by the group, perhaps at the first full meeting of the committee. At this point, the director, who has acted as facilitator, may step down from that role, or may assume the leadership role. The smaller the library, the better chance the director will quite naturally become the leader. The larger the group, or the more mixed its participants are, the better the chance that a leader will arise who is not the director, but perhaps a member of the board, Friends' group, or even a patron with the kind of personality that others follow. It may be necessary to wait until the second meeting to see if a leader emerges from the group. The natural leader may be the library director or deputy director, who, in the role of facilitator at the beginning of the first meeting, was seen to bring out the best in people. It may be better not to vote or select a leader too quickly. Whoever is selected should want the position because of the contribution to the process that he or she can make, not for their own ideas for the product.

An effective leader should share the authority of the committee with the members of that committee. The basic philosophy of leadership should be to assist members to work effectively together and to build a group capable of regulating and developing itself. A leader should serve and assist. By the second meeting, however, a leader should have been identified by the way in which that person acts within the group as a whole. If this does not happen, the best choice for a leader is the individual who is the best facilitator.

For the group process to work, everyone in the group must feel equal. All committee members must be encouraged to speak, listen, and continue to discuss until a consensus is reached about the various points along the way. Without the free exchange of ideas, thoughts, values, and principles, you have no group process. The group process is not easy. Do not despair. In the beginning there are going to be some problems. The more you solve at the beginning, the better the process you will have throughout, and the better decision making at the end. Some common problems that may assail the group include:

- quitting too soon,
- collecting too much information and then not knowing what to do with it,
- enjoying the process and not wanting to get to the conclusion.

The process is the key to success. The end product depends greatly on the ability of the group to function well. Ideas for collection development must come from many sectors of the community, not just the professionals. It is the idea behind this that makes the process so important. It is only through this process that ideas are generated. In developing the product, ideas are solidified; if there are not enough ideas, the product will be empty. The most important thing to do in every process is to start. At this juncture, that is the next step.

GETTING STARTED

To get things going, provide each subcommittee (if you have them) or the committee as a whole with sufficient background reading so they can begin to think about their library in relation to what others have written on the subject. A list of suggested readings can be found at the end of this chapter. Then break down the larger topic into a series of smaller topics for the sake of focusing the discussion. An example of a topic that is too large is the community analysis project. Instead of talking about the community as a whole, how about spending some time on the residential neighborhoods that make up the community, learning about the ethnic groups, the jobs performed, the family units, the children's ages, the financial outlook, etc. For another discussion, choose the commercial neighborhoods and discuss who owns and runs the businesses in the community, where they live, who they are, what kind of a commitment they have to the community, what their clubs, lodges, and leisure time activities are. There are any number of ways to look at a community, but the most interesting are a glance at the people who make up the area. As each part of the discussion is completed, someone from the group should be assigned to write up the results of the discussion. In chapter 3 we will start collecting information and evaluating it.

REFERENCES

Most of these references are practical, how-to-do-it kinds of materials. For more recent ones, or to find out if these are still in print, look at *Subject Guide to Books in Print* under "Meetings," "Social Groups," or "Group Relations Training."

Bertcher, Harvey J., and Maple, Frank F. *Creating Groups*. Beverly Hills, Calif.: Sage Publishing, 1977.

Bradford, Leland. *Making Meetings Work: A Guide For Leaders and Group Members*. San Diego, Calif.: University Associates, 1976.

Callahan, Joseph A. *Communicating—How to Organize Meetings and Presentations*. New York: Franklin Watts, 1984.

Creth, Sheila. *Conducting Effective Meetings and Other Time Management Techniques*. Chicago: Association of College and Research Libraries, 1982.

Doyle, Michael and Straus, David. *How to Make Meetings Work*. New York: Jove Publications, 1986.

Hackman, J. Richard, ed. *Groups that Work (& Those That Don't): Creating Conditions for Effective Teamwork*. New York: Jossey-Bass, 1989.

Hyman, Ronald T. *Improving Discussion Leadership*. New York: Columbia University Teachers College Press, 1980.

King, James P. *How to Run Effective Meetings*. Wilton, Conn.: Brown House, 1986.

Palmer, Barbara C., and Palmer, Kenneth R. *The Successful Meeting*. Englewood Cliffs, N.J.: Prentice-Hall, 1983.

Renton, Michael. *Getting Better Results from the Meetings You Run*. Champaign, Ill.: Research Press, 1980.

Shindler-Rainman, Eva and Lippitt, Ronald. *Taking Your Meeting Out of the Doldrums*. La Jolla, Calif.: University Associates, 1977.

Tropman, John E. *Effective Meetings: Improving Group Decision-Making*. Beverly Hills, Calif.: Sage Publications, 1980.

———. *Meetings: How to Make them Work for You*. New York: Van Nostrand Reinhold, 1984.

Stone, Julia M. *How to Work with Groups: Guidelines for Volunteers*. La Crescenta, Calif.: C.C. Thomas, 1983.

Wood, Douglas, and Phillips, Gerald M. *Group Discussions: A Practical Guide to Participation and Leadership*. 2nd ed. New York: Harper and Row, 1985.

3 THE LIBRARY AND ITS COLLECTIONS

The first step in a successful collection development process is to gather information on, and evaluate the current status of, two elements: the library and its community. In chapter four we'll discuss the community. Here we'll cover the library—its collection, procedures, and staff. Gathering information will reveal the status of the library's collection as well as the changes that need to be made. It is necessary to gather information on all aspects of the library's collection and procedures which could in any way impinge on collection development. This is the starting point for deciding how to develop the collection for the future.

There are six basic areas that should be addressed: staff, the collection itself, budget, hours and usage, the arrangement of materials, and the collection of statistics and related data.

STAFF

It goes without saying that a library depends very heavily on the people who work there. Staff members are an important source of information about the library's collection and about how the collection is used. Their knowledge and expertise can be used in the development of the collection. Each staff member—whether working in a clerical capacity, as a librarian, as a public relations person, or as an administrator—should be interviewed to determine past and present duties, interests inside and outside the library, educational background, other jobs they have held, or knowledge their family members may have about the library and its collection that might be useful in the process of collection development. Figure 3-1 is an example of an interview form which could be used to gather this information.

Establish who is now involved in collection development—either formally assigned to it or participating informally through suggestions to those who are. Examine the potential levels of participation by evaluating each staff member's educational qualifications, skills, and any possible untapped expertise which could be utilized in collection development—whether it is expertise for selecting books, periodicals, audiovisual materials, or computer software; or expertise in a certain subject area such as how to run a small business, early childhood education, or personal finance. Then make a chart by subject area and by type of material to determine what coverage you have and what gaps remain. The chart might look like Figure 3-2.

FIGURE 3-1 STAFF INTERVIEW FORM

Name_____

Present position in the Library _____

Job responsibilities _____

List previous positions and responsibilities of those positions

_____

_____

_____

Educational background. Please list academic institutions

attended and degrees earned._____

_____

Other work experience (outside the Library). Please describe

each position briefly._____

_____

_____

Hobbies and Interests. Please list._____

_____

Memberships in local, state and national organizations. Please

list. _____

_____

_____

Community activities such as volunteer work. Please list.

_____

FIGURE 3-2 LIBRARY BOOK SELECTION ASSIGNMENTS

SUBJECT	DEWEY NO.	STAFF MEMBER	SCOPE
Computers	001.65 - 005.99	B. White	Beginning and intermediate level
Philosophy	100 - 129	Open	Basic level
Psychology	150 - 159	T. Eagle	Basic level with emphasis on self help
Religion	200 - 299	J. Johnston	Basic level

Ask staff how they see the library's collection, include both its strengths and weaknesses. They may have noticed some details about the status of the collection and what needs to be done to improve it that others have overlooked. In some areas the library may need to assign two people to keep up with the amount of material needed. In other areas there may be little need to buy, and someone can easily assume the collection development responsibilities with little impact on their work load.

In interviewing staff members, you may also uncover problems in library procedures which affect collection development or which impact on the library's ability to deliver books to the library's users in a timely fashion. For example, you may discover that even though books are ordered in a timely fashion, there is inadequate staff to process and catalog new books. As a result borrowers have to wait three or four weeks before the books are available. Or, you may learn that there is no coordination between new purchases, reserve requests, and interlibrary loan requests. In this case many titles may be requested repeatedly but not ordered.

COLLECTION OF STATISTICS

Statistics are an important point of reference for decision making. It is therefore important that sufficient data—and the right kind of data—are gathered on a regular basis. The following sections will discuss in some detail the kinds of statistics which can be useful to you in formulating a collection development policy and in monitoring the development and use of the collection.

CIRCULATION

Circulation statistics are of great importance to writing and organizing the collection development policy. These figures can tell you a great deal about the use of the library's collection. They can tell you what parts of the collection circulate best and what parts seldom circulate. They can tell you whether children or adults check out the most books and provide you with other trends in library use. Is the circulation of fiction declining and the circulation of nonfiction increasing? Is the circulation of children's books increasing at a faster rate than the circulation of adult materials?

If you have an automated circulation system, you'll be able to gather monthly statistics on:

- the number of books that have circulated by subject areas such as the 620s or the 790s
- the number of books that have circulated by age level, i.e., adult books, young adult books, juvenile books,
- the number of books circulated by characteristics of users—level of education, language preferred, age, residence (part of town, a nearby town, a suburb, etc.),
- the circulation by kind of material—books, paperbacks, magazines, audiovisual materials (audiocassettes, videos, CDs, etc.),
- the variations in circulation by the month of the year.

The statistical report is produced each month by the automated circulation system. The kind of statistics to be collected should be determined at the time the automated system is being planned. The library should decide what materials categories it needs. For example, do you want certain Dewey numbers broken down smaller than in 10s such as the 390s which includes folklore as well as etiquette or is it sufficient to know how many 390s circulate. Smaller breakdowns can be useful since you'll be able to tell in more detail what your users are borrowing. The demographics for users can also prove most interesting. It's worth having your patrons fill out a form that—at a minimum—indicates the language they prefer, their age, and where they live (by part of town). Later on you'll be able to tell more about who your patrons are and better determine their needs. You will also be able to tell who doesn't use the library. Figure 3-3 is an example of the kind of statistics produced by an automated system. (See Solesz's article for more information on using the automated circulation system for collection development.)

If the statistics are being collected in your library manually, you should be able to obtain the following:

- the number of adult, young adult, and children's books circulated by category.
- the number of books that have circulated monthly in each subject area, i.e., 590s, 810s, and 940s;
- the kind of material circulated: books, recordings, picture books, CDs, audiocassettes, videocassettes, etc.;
- the variations in circulation by month of the year.

Figures 3-4 and 3-5 are examples of forms used to keep circulation statistics with a manual circulation system. Note that nonfiction categories can be broken down into smaller units, i.e., 110, 120, 130, 140, etc. They should also be expanded to include young adult and children's circulation.

Circulation statistics will tell you what subject areas are most in demand and most often checked out; who the library is serving in broad terms; what kind of materials circulate the most; and the variations by the month of the year.

Using this data you'll be able to identify patterns and look at how your materials are being used. How does this vary from one subject to another? If people in the community are taking graduate courses at a nearby university, it may explain why a particular subject area does well. Or maybe a large number of people work in jobs where they can retire early which results in some using the job and career materials to look for a second career and others using the library a great deal for entertainment. Some of the information you collect in your community study will fit with this data to explain your circulation statistics. This data will be useful in

FIGURE 3-3 MONTHLY CIRCULATION STATISTICS -- AUTOMATED SYSTEM

<u>**MATERIALS**</u>

Circulation   **Circulation Classes**

Circulation	Class	Description
2,293	FIC	General Fiction
690	FIC	Mysteries
94	FIC	Science Fiction
15	000 - 099	Generalities
30	001.65 - 005.99	Computers
5	100 - 129	Philosophy, Theory
21	130 - 139	Paranormal Phenomena
42	150 - 159	Psychology

<u>**USERS**</u>

Number   **Description**

Number	Description
30	Edgewater, English, 8 - 11 years*
19	Edgewater, English, 12 - 18 years
137	Edgewater, English, 19 - 64 years
43	Edgewater. English, 65 years & ups
7	Edgewater. Chinese, 19 - 65 years
4	Edgewater, Russian, 65 years & up
18	Edgewater, Spanish, 12 - 18 years
124	Edgewater, Spanish, 19 - 64 years

*These user statistics indicate the name of the community of the user, the language the user prefers to read, and the age category.

FIGURE 3-4 DAILY AND WEEKLY CIRCULATION RECORD

WEEK_____

CATEGORY		MON	TUES	WED	THURS	FRI	SAT	SUN	TOTAL
Generalities	000								
Philosophy	100								
Religion	200								
Social Sciences	300								
Language	400								
Pure Sciences	500								
Technology	600								
The Arts	700								
Literature	800								
History	900-909								
	930-999								
Geography, Travel	910-919								
Collective Biography	920-929								
Biography	92 or B								
Total Adult Nonfiction									
Adult Fiction									
Adult Paperbacks									
Total Adult Book Circulation									
Periodicals									
Pamphlets									
Audiocassettes									
Videocassettes									
CDs									
Computer Software									
Other									
TOTAL ADULT CIRCULATION									

FIGURE 3-5 MONTHLY CIRCULATION RECORD

MONTH/YEAR_____

CATEGORY		CURRENT	PREVIOUS YEAR	INCREASE/DECREASE
Generalities	000			
Philosophy	100			
Religion	200			
Social Sciences	300			
Language	400			
Pure Sciences	500			
Technology	600			
The Arts	700			
Literature	800			
History	900-909			
	930-999			
Geography, Travel	910-919			
Collective Biography	920-929			
Biography	92 or B			
Total Adult Nonfiction				
Adult Fiction				
Adult Paperbacks				
Total Adult Book Circulation				
Periodicals				
Pamphlets				
Audiocassettes				
Videocassettes				
CDs				
Computer Software				
Other				
TOTAL ADULT CIRCULATION				

formulating your collection development policy since it will be one important barometer of usage and interests.

RESERVES

A fast, interesting, and useful way to analyze the success or failure of your collection is to look at reserves and see how long it takes to get material to a patron. Also look at what titles and/or subject areas are not purchased by the library. This can be accomplished by taking an in-house survey or by interviewing patrons. An analysis of reserves may highlight the need for more newly published materials and/or copies of older titles. It may also lead to a change in reserve policy. How many reserves should be taken before multiple copies of material are ordered.

Here are some guidelines for studying reserves. Take a look at the number of reserves for titles on the best seller list versus the number of copies available. Then determine whether the number of copies you have will enable the user to get the reserve in a reasonable period of time. Use the form in Figure 3-6. You might pick a week and take a sample of the reserves received on each day (10 percent of those received or more if the number is small). Find out how many are presently available in the library and on order. Track them for three months and see what percentage has been filled. You could do this by flagging certain reserves in an unautomated system or identifying the reserve in some special way in an automated system. This will give you a good idea of how well you are meeting your patrons' requests. Unless the book is still not published, the reserve should have been filled either by the library or through interlibrary loan. There will, of course, be exceptions in the case of runaway best-sellers. But three months seems a reasonable time for filling most reserves.

If you want to interview patrons, then you should develop a few short questions to ask. The survey should be taken over the same three-month period. You could interview 20 people a day for a total of five days using the questionnaire in Figure 3-7 Record their experience with reserves and if they are satisfied with the fulfillment time and ability to get the materials requested. If you find many unsatisfied users, it will be another piece of information you will want to fit into your collection development policy and the procedures emanating from it.

REFERENCE

Reference statistics are invaluable when working on collection development. Since reference questions reveal a great deal about the need for information and materials in all subject areas, some

---

FIGURE 3-6 RESERVE REQUESTS

DATE_____

TITLE	NO. COPIES	NO. RESERVES	COMMENTS
Millie Speaks	3	25	Buy 2 more copies
The Good Life	1	6	Buy 1 more copy
World of Politics	6	26	No problem

---

libraries keep a record of each question asked. A separate list is kept of those questions that could not be answered from the collection, in order to signal subject area weaknesses. Many libraries also record questions referred to other libraries or the network reference office.

Study the data collected as another way to pinpoint weaknesses. For instance, one library's survey of reference questions indicated that there were many questions about computer software that the library's reference staff was unable to answer. Material constantly had to be obtained for users through interlibrary loan. As a result, the head librarian noted that the library needed to add more books on software and computer magazines to the collection.

At another library many people suddenly started asking questions about investments. It was discovered that there was little material available on the topic that had been published in the last two years. Again, the librarian became aware that the library needed to add more circulating materials on investments, some

FIGURE 3-7 RESERVE SYSTEM QUESTIONNAIRE

PLEASE TAKE A FEW MINUTES AND HELP US IMPROVE OUR RESERVE SYSTEM.

Do you request that books be reserved for you?

_____yes _____no

How often do make requests for reserves?

____ once a week   ____ once every two weeks

____ once a month   ____ at least four times a year

____ infrequently

Do you usually get the books you reserve?

_____yes _____no

If not, have you inquired as to why you never received the books?

_____yes _____no

How quickly do you usually get a reserve book?

____ in a week   ____ in two weeks

____ in a month   ____ in two months

____ in three to six months

Do you think that the amount of time you wait is reasonable?

_____yes _____no

Do you have any comments or suggestions concerning reserves?

_____

_____

reference material, and discard the out-of-date material. Still another library traced the level of questions not being answered and learned that more books on higher levels of mathematics and more basic works of literary criticism for use by high school students were needed.

Figure 3-8 can be used for keeping reference statistics that will provide you with quite a bit of information without your staff spending an unreasonable amount of time on record keeping. With this form staff members can make a mark for each question they handle checking the level of the question—ready reference, reference, or research. As time permits, they can add some comments or note specific questions they could not answer. These sheets should be examined weekly by someone in the reference department to identify problem areas and work on filling gaps in the collection.

IN-HOUSE USE OF MATERIALS

Another way to measure how the collection is being used is to evaluate how materials (both circulating and reference) are used in-house by patrons. The best way to do this is to periodically post signs and ask patrons not to reshelve materials. This could be done once a week for a month. Have the pages collect all materials left on the tables hourly and count by call number (Dewey Decimal or Library of Congress) what has been collected before reshelving. Figure 3-9 is a form which can be used for this activity. The number of books collected each hour can simply be recorded in the appropriate space depending on their call number and time of day.

TECHNICAL SERVICES

Statistics from technical services—the number of materials ordered and processed—will show you the library's present buying patterns. Many libraries keep statistics on the number of new materials cataloged in each section of the classification system. They then compare the annual publishing output in a subject area with the library's acquisitions and holdings in those same subject area. See Figure 3-10.

You can do this by compiling the following statistics:

- the annual publishing output in a subject as found in *Publishers Weekly* or the *Bowker Annual*,
- the number of books and other materials bought during the year on a subject (see chart at the end of this section to record your library's purchases,)
- the median age of material in a subject area,

FIGURE 3-8 REFERENCE STATISTICS

DATE_____

SUBJECT*		READY REF.	REFERENCE	RESEARCH	TOTAL
Generalities Computers	000				
Philosophy Psychology	100				
Religion Mythology	200				

Social Sciences
   Business/Economics
   Education
	300				

Language	400				
Pure Sciences	500				

Technology
   Gardening
   Medicine/Health
   Cooking
   Home Repair
	600				

The Arts
   Art/Photography
   Crafts/Hobbies
   Music
   Recreation/Sports
	700				

Literature	800				
History	900-909 930-999				
Geography/Travel	910-919				
Biography	920-929				
TOTAL					

Notes on unanswered questions _____
_____

*Categories can be changed to fit your library's needs.

FIGURE 3-9 IN-HOUSE USE OF LIBRARY MATERIALS

DATE_____

CATEGORIES*	TIME OF DAY**								
	9-10	10-11	11-12	12-1	1-2	2-3	3-4	4-5	5-6
000 - 099									
100 - 199									
200 - 299									
300 - 399									
400 - 499									
500 - 599									
600 - 699									
700 - 799									
800 - 899									
900 - 999									
Fiction									
Periodicals									
Paperbacks									
A-V Materials									
TOTAL									

*Expand the categories to fit your library. You may also want to have a separate chart for children's or young adult materials.

**Alter the times to fit your library's hours.

FIGURE 3-10 LIBRARY BUYING POWER

SUBJECT	NO. TITLES PUBLISHED	NO. NEW TITLES*	MEDIAN AGE OF TITLES**	NO OF NEW TITLES AVAIL***
Business	1,647	30	1987	7

* This is the number of new titles the Library has purchased in the current year.

** This is the median age of the titles in this subject area owned by the Library.

*** This is the number of new titles on the shelf at the time of the spot check.

- the amount of new material purchased which remains on the shelves. (Do spot checks of the shelves periodically to get this number. This will tie in with the circulation figures kept, too.)

You'll want to analyze these figures in conjunction with the circulation in the subject area—in this case, business. If the circulation is high, as would seem to be indicated by the small number of new books on the shelf, then you'll want to note in your collection development policy that this area of the collection needs to be emphasized. Since the median age of this part of the collection seems a bit old in relation to the changing ideas in this field, there should be an effort made to increase the amount of new material purchased and an effort to weed some items which are out-of-date. The publishing output indicates that a wide range of material is being published on that subject. If each subject area is analyzed in this way, you will get a picture of what the library's strengths and weaknesses are.

The form in Figure 3-11 will be useful in showing how many new titles are being purchased in each subject area.

BUDGET

The budget is a good indication of the library's present priorities and policies. For example, the line-item budget will provide details by format—books, periodicals, pamphlets, videos, recordings, audiocassettes; age level—adults, young adults, children; subjects—religion, astronomy, psychology; and genre—fiction, nonfiction, and reference.

You will need to collect information about the library's present budget and spending patterns. You can use the budget worksheet in Figure 3-2. You will want information on how the materials budget is spent—the amount for children's materials, young adult materials, adult materials, large-print materials, reference materials, and periodicals. You will also want to know the amount spent for audiovisual materials such as audiocassettes, videos, compact disks, and computer software, as well as for some of the older formats which the community will still want. Is the budget sufficient to buy what the users want or is there a period near the end of the fiscal year when few titles can be ordered? You'll also want to know the relationship between the amount of new materials purchased and replacements, as well as the relationship between the number of hardcovers and paperbacks purchased. Compare the library's budget and spending information with the information that has been collected about the community. Does the spending pattern reinforce the information collected? If there is a growing number of senior citizens in the community, has your budget for large-print books increased? Has the number of families with young children increased and has the size of the children's collection increased as well? Your collection development policy should reflect the information collected about the budget and the community which may, in fact, change the library's buying patterns.

The proportion of the materials collection spent on different age levels should reflect both usage and the proportion in different age groups in the community. As audiovisual materials become increasingly popular, this part of the budget will increase to meet community demand. The periodical budget will reflect the varied interests of the community.

FIGURE 3-11 NEW TITLES

CATEGORIES*

MONTH_____

NUMBER OF TITLES PURCHASED

000 - 099

100 - 199

200 - 299

300 - 399

400 - 499

500 - 599

600 - 699

700 - 799

800 - 899

900 - 999

Fiction

TOTAL

*You will want to break these large categories down into smaller
ones to fit your library (i.e. 910, 920, 930, etc.) and have a
separate sheet for young adult materials and one for children's
materials.

In one rural library, cable television had not become available and so videos were very important. Since many first-run movies and foreign films come out very quickly in video, the library began to fund its audiovisual collection at a higher level. It also purchased a variety of documentary videos.

You'll want to look at other parts of your budget. Look at the staffing budget to see if it is adequate for handling materials selection and the processing and cataloging of materials when they arrive. Most libraries provide enough staff for public service functions such as reference and the circulation desk and to handle routine daily matters, but disregard the need to order new materials, fill in collection gaps; and weed the collection.

Look at the equipment budget to see if the library is allotting enough money for items such as new shelving, microfilm readers and reader-printers, storage and display units for videos and audiotapes. Also is there money for equipment for the public to use in the library, such as VCRs, compact disk players, and personal computers. These factors are all related to the use of the collection.

Use the budget worksheet, Figure 3-12, to collect and analyze budget information.

HOURS AND USAGE

If your library is open a limited number of hours, only certain segments of the community will be able to use the library. This, of course, is reflected in the collection's use. Therefore, the hours of service have a direct impact on collection development.

You may want to study usage patterns to determine how people use the library and when they use it. To get a good sample, study usage for one week every other month for a year. Figure 3-13 can be used by your staff to record the data.

From this data you will discover when the library is less used and when it is most used. You may even want to try some different hours of opening as a result of the survey.

ARRANGEMENT OF MATERIALS

You will need to gather information about the arrangement of materials particularly from the user's point of view. Pretend you are a new user and try to observe the library with a fresh eye. Look at whether it is easy for patrons to orient themselves when they enter the library. Look at whether the books are arranged so that it is easy to follow the numerical sequence of the collection. If a section of books is not in the place the user would expect to find it, it is possible that section is not used as well as it should be. Over a period of two months walk around the library on a regular basis to note what sections of the collection seem to be little used. Then

---

FIGURE 3-12 BUDGET WORKSHEET

CATEGORY	CURRENT YR.	PREVIOUS YR.	INCREASE	COMMENTS
Books*				
Periodicals				
A-V Material*				
Fringe Benefits				
Health Insurance				
Social Security				
Retirement Plan				
Electricity				
Gas				
Telephone				
Postage				
Building Maintenance				
Equipment				
Supplies				
Travel				
Computer Expenses				

*You will want to break these two categories down into smaller units as discussed in the text for purposes of monitoring your expenditures.

FIGURE 3-13 USAGE PATTERNS

DATE_____

HOURS   **NUMBER OF PEOPLE IN LIBRARY**

	MON	TUES	WED	THURS	FRI	SAT	SUN	TOTAL
9 - 10								
10 - 11								
11 - 12								
12 - 1								
1 - 2								
2 - 3								
3 - 4								
4 - 5								
5 - 6								
6 - 7								
7 - 8								
8 - 9								
TOTAL								

note whether these are sections which might be out of sequence and thus difficult to find. For instance, genre books are often shelved separately; it can simply be a matter of judgment whether a book ends up in the genre section or in the fiction section. Or if a local history section is in a special location (out of numerical sequence), someone just following the regular numerical sequence could miss that section, unless the signage is well done and the shelves are carefully marked.

You may wonder why the arrangement of the collection is

discussed in a manual on collection development, but the arrangement affects the use of the collection. Sometimes parts of the collection go unused simply because the collection is badly arranged and marked. Often oversized books are shelved separately and are never used. Also, libraries tend to pull out parts of a reference collection and shelve them separately often forgetting to mark these changes in the catalog or on the shelf itself. Look over the collection carefully and ask a friend or two to give you an outsider's opinion. You may be surprised at how a few well-placed signs will increase the use of particular parts of the collection or how some face-out shelving will increase usage of books that seldom circulated previously. Use the form in Figure 3-14 for your walk around the library.

THE COLLECTION

A detailed examination of the current collection is at the heart of preparing a collection development plan. You will want to find out what your collection really looks like and whether it fits the library's goals and objectives—especially whether it meets the needs of your patrons.

INVENTORY

Just as the staff was a good place to start when looking at your library's procedures and practices, an inventory is one starting point to examine the collection; because it documents your library's actual holdings. Doing an inventory involves comparing the shelf list to the shelves—title by title and copy by copy—with follow-up for books that were in circulation when the inventory was done. It can be done in sections or all at one time. While the library can remain open, it is preferable to do the inventory when it is closed. This way the staff will not interrupt the patrons and can devote full time to the project.

Use all the staff—clerical staff, pages, and custodial staff—for this project. They can do a good job with minimal supervision. If you don't have sufficient staff, consider contracting with a company that does this work. These companies often advertise in library periodicals and exhibit at library conferences. Depending on your timing and funding, this can be a very practical solution since you don't have to hire and train the staff yourself.

Once you have finished the inventory, you will have a better idea

FIGURE 3-14 WALK AROUND SURVEY

Name of Library _____ Date _____

1. When you enter the building can you quickly orient
yourself?

2. Are there signs directing you to the various departments
of the library?

3. Are the stacks accurately labeled?

4. Is it easy to follow the nonfiction section? Is the
arrangement logical?

5. If any of the nonfiction is out of sequence, is there a
sign on the shelf where it should be indicating where it is
located?

6. Is the reference section easy to use? If sections are
out of order, is there a sign on the shelf where it should
be indicating where it is located?

7. Can you find the audiovisual section?

8. Can you find the children's section?

9. Can you find the young adult section?

10. Can you find the periodicals?

of what gaps you have in your collection. Are many standard titles missing? Do you have many copies of old best-sellers that never circulate? Have certain subject areas been depleted? You may determine that the reason certain subject areas have a low circulation is the insufficient material available. Your inventory results will provide an important piece of information for your collection development plan.

COLLECTION EVALUATION

Once the inventory is completed, you can begin your collection evaluation, during which you'll be noting out-of-date material, duplicates no longer needed, physical decay, and books which need to be either rebound or replaced—in addition to comparing your holdings against generally accepted standards. The standard catalog series published by H.W. Wilson Company includes two catalogs of value to public libraries. The *Public Library Catalog* and the *Fiction Catalog*. You can compare your library's holdings against the titles and subjects in other lists, as well. Some examples are *Good Reading* (R.R. Bowker Co.); the *Reader's Advisor* (R.R. Bowker Co.); and the *Reader's Catalog, An Annotated Selection of More Than 40,000 of the Best Books in Print in 208 Categories.* Guides to the literature of a particular time period may be helpful as well as guides to historical fiction, to genre fiction, annual best books lists by subject area in *Library Journal, Booklist,* etc., and lists published by large public libraries such as the Enoch Pratt Free Library in Baltimore and the New York Public Library. In the audiovisual area there are not as many evaluative sources but those available will be discussed in the audiovisual section.

Collection evaluation will enable you to pinpoint which standard works are owned, missing, or never purchased. A note of caution about standard lists: they include a limited selection of books and may omit as many good titles as they include. Do not use them solely for identifying items not in your library's collection. Use them to make sure that you are not missing any important areas, that you are buying high quality materials, a representative selection of authors, and subjects which will fit the needs of your community.

EVALUATING THE FICTION COLLECTION

In evaluating the fiction collection use all the information you have collected about circulation, reserves, and current buying patterns and use them in conjunction with the standard bibliographical guides and a physical examination of the shelves. However, the first thing you will want to do is to compare your fiction collection to the *Fiction Catalog* and to any other lists you have chosen. The ALA *Notable Books* lists for the last few years is one obvious source. Most libraries do not have all the books listed in *Fiction Catalog* but do have a representative selection of books by important writers. You can check the titles listed in the *Fiction Catalog* against other lists such as *Good Reading, Reader's Catalog, 80 Years of Best Sellers, Genreflecting, American Historical Fiction* and the *Reader's Advisor*, as well as genre bibliographies such as *Anatomy of Wonder* and *Crime Fiction*, to help determine whether you have an author's best works.

Then look at the results of your inventory to see which recommended titles that you once owned are missing from your collection. You may also want to find out if you have many little-read titles on your shelves or duplicates of former best-sellers which are no longer read. This can be determined by looking to see if a book has been circulating. You can do a random sample; check every tenth book, then check the shelf list against circulation records or the stamped date due slip. If, for example, it is discovered in this check that every fourth book examined has not gone out of the library in over five years, it means that approximately 25 percent of the collection has not been used in a very long time. One explanation is little interest in the community for older titles. Further checking should be done. With an automated circulation system you can run a list of titles that have not circulated within a specified time period. Look at the circulation figures to see how fiction does in relation to the number of titles available—both the number of new fiction titles and the number of retrospective ones. Then look at the shelves again. If there are older titles on the shelf while the newer works are in circulation, it indicates that the library should be buying more current titles. If both the newer and older titles circulate, it should be kept in mind that the fiction section needs a good retrospective collection.

Fiction is the most difficult area of the collection to evaluate. You'll want to use a great deal of care in deciding which titles should be replaced. A library does need to have the classics because they represent a basic core collection that is read by generation after generation, as well as important pivotal works, most of the major writers, and as large a collection of new fiction titles by contemporary writers as possible—both those published by major presses and those by small presses. Replace first titles which are deemed important and have been noted as missing in the inventory. Replace other titles selectively keeping in mind that older fiction titles are read less than current fiction.

Other types of literature which share the same sort of criteria for evaluation as fiction include plays, essays and poetry—works of imagination and creativity. These works do not date because of the subject matter, but rather because of popularity of style or author, social significance, and use. In one library the librarian after checking these collections against the *Public Library Catalog* and *The Reader's Advisor* discovered that the library had purchased few volumes of American poetry written after 1975. So the librarian noting that these sections received a moderate amount of use began to order the works of some contemporary American poets as noted in these guides and to read the book review media with an eye to adding to this part of the collection.

EVALUATING THE NONFICTION COLLECTION

The nonfiction collection is somewhat easier to evaluate than the fiction collection. Here you will want to check the shelves against standard tools, look at the circulation statistics for that subject, and look at rate of loss as identified by the inventory. Analyze each subject area on an individual basis using the form in figure 3-15. You can probably use the tens of Dewey (i.e., 530, 540, 550, etc.) but in some cases slightly larger or smaller groupings will be more appropriate. You will want to compare the number of new titles in the library's collection to the activity in a particular field, the rate of change of information in the field in relation to the number of new titles and new editions available, the annual publishing output in that field, and whether that output indicates a great deal of new information or just greater interest in that subject.

You might want to expand your information gathering to an evaluation of the levels of materials gathered and the depth of collecting in a subject area. The four levels of collection development, which are defined in chapter five, are popular, general information, instructional, and reference. The library chooses to collect at different levels for different subject areas depending on the demand for material in that area and the kinds of patrons using these materials. Therefore, in this evaluation of subject areas, the librarian might want to note what level of material is most used. This can be done by choosing a few basic titles on the subject and a few more scholarly titles on the same subject and comparing their circulation.

If you have information on reserves at this point, it could be helpful. Do reserves pile up for particular titles? Sometimes there are titles in addition to new books, for which there are a steady number of requests. Many standard titles are frequently reserved, as well as nonstandard titles, because of their subject. Look for missing titles or titles repeatedly requested.

FIGURE 3-15 WORKSHEET FOR EVALUATING NONFICTION

Subject _____

Rate of Change in the Field

_____ slow
_____ moderate
_____ fast

Lists Used for Evaluating Subject _____

_____

_____

Does This Subject Area Need Weeding?

_____ yes
_____ no

Is There Enough Material to Meet the Demand?

_____ yes
_____ no

What Level of Material Circulates the Most?

_____ popular
_____ general information
_____ instructional
_____ reference

Are Replacements Needed?

_____ yes
_____ no

Is Enough New Material Being Purchased?

_____ yes
_____ no

Recommendations_____

_____

In one library the librarian assigned to evaluate the health and medicine section began by checking the collection against the *Public Library Catalog* realizing that in this fast-changing field even some of the titles listed would be too old. But she felt it would give her an overview of what kinds of material needed to be included and in some cases she could check for newer editions of the books listed. She also used a recent list of books she found in *Library Journal*. In a cursory look at the shelves in this section, she found that the books circulated frequently and that few new titles were ever on the shelves. In fact some titles, which were too old to be of much value, also circulated. The circulation statistics for this area indicated that each title was circulating an average of five times a year. The inventory indicated that a number of fairly recent titles were missing. Although a large number of books on medicine are published each year, many are too technical for public libraries so the choices are somewhat limited. From this evaluation the librarian noted that the library needed to acquire more new material than it had in the past and sometimes even buy two copies of important titles to meet the demand for health and medical material.

SPECIAL COLLECTIONS

Special collections owned by the library need to be evaluated by the library staff. There may be a local history collection, a local authors' collection and other special collections. They should be examined for completeness, for excessive duplication, and for usage. If a bibliographic guide for the subject area exists, the collection should be checked against that guide. Sometimes local history is spread among several local institutions, which may include town government and the local historical society. The librarian will want to examine all the collections to see how they differ and how they duplicate each other. They may need more coordination than they have had in the past. All may lack certain basic materials; if this is so, some attempt can be made to acquire them.

AUDIOVISUAL MATERIALS

Audiovisual materials include recordings, compact disks, audiotapes, videos, slides, and computer software. This is an important area to evaluate since it is growing rapidly. The evaluation should include checking the collection against standard lists that include Halsey's *Classical Music Recordings for Home and Library* (ALA) and *The New Penguin Guide to Compact Discs and Cassettes* (Penguin) for classical recordings and CDs, and *On Cassette, A Comprehensive*

Bibliography of Spoken-Word Audio Cassettes (Bowker) for audio cassettes. For videos there are several including *Halliwell's Film and Video Guide, Video for Libraries: Special Interest Video for Small and Medium-Sized Public Libraries*, ed. by Sally Mason and James Scholtz (ALA, 1988), *Developing and Maintaining Video Collections in Libraries*, by James C. Scholtz (ABC-Clio, 1989), *Movies on TV and Videocassette*, ed. by Steven H. Scheuer (Bantam, annual), and *Leonard Maltin's TV Movies and Video Guide* (New American Library, annual). With nonprint there is also a need to acquire retrospective items as has been done in the rest of the collection.

Next, look at the circulation statistics to evaluate the popularity of each format. If possible, do a sampling of the usage of each format so you can evaluate the kinds of material which circulate best. Also check the shelves periodically to see what items are always on the shelves and what items are never there. For example, in one library many of the education-related videos seldom circulated while the feature films were never on the shelves. Look at the results of the inventory to see what items are missing from the collection. Evaluate how well your collection has been developed in relation to what is available. Do you buy a wide range of subjects? This may also cause you to look at recent review media to get a better idea of what kinds of material are being produced. You may also want to look at which subjects circulate well in the book collection and evaluate whether there is a need for supplementary material in audio or video formats.

PERIODICALS

In some subject areas magazines serve as the only source of recent information. For example, in the computer field current information is available only in periodicals; information is usually dated by the time a book is published. It's important to evaluate the use of magazines in your library in order to ascertain whether you have developed a collection that meets your community's needs. You can check your collection against information provided in Katz's *Magazines for Libraries*, which provides guidelines for the most important periodical acquisitions by subject area. You can also compare your book circulation with your periodical collection. Do you have periodicals to support the most popular parts of your book collection—particularly if these are areas where information changes rapidly. You can also include magazines in your in-house survey. Have the pages put a small sticker on each magazine found on a table so later you can look at the magazines and tell which

IN SUMMARY, REMEMBER:
—staff members are an important source of information,
—statistics need to be gathered on a regular basis to support decision making,
—the budget is a good indicator of the library's priorities,
—hours and the arrangement of materials affect usage,
—evaluate your current collection as you prepare a collection development plan.

were used. Finally look at the circulation of magazines to see how well they circulate.

PUBLISHING TRENDS

It's important to keep up with publishing trends so that you can foresee new developments and plan accordingly. For example, there is a trend to publish original paperbacks (a cheaper format for the publisher), especially for fiction. Most libraries usually prefer hardcover books because they are more durable and many collection development policies once said that paperbacks were not recommended if hardcovers were available. However, now that paperbacks are nearly as expensive and hardcover books are less durable, this stipulation has changed.

Publishers Weekly is the major source of information on publishing trends for publishers, it also serves librarians well. It publishes annual statistics (included in the *Bowker Annual*), articles on specialized publishing, for instance, religious publishing, and news on individual books. One of its most important articles is published in the fall and entitled ''Titles and Prices, 19XX, Final Figures,'' which gives both the average prices of books for the year by category and tells how many titles were published in each category.

Now that you have collected as much data as possible on the library's collection, you may want to put it into a capsule form so that you'll have a summary document. The chart in Figure 3-16 is for summarizing the information you have collected. The interpretation of this information will depend somewhat on the library— its goals and objectives. In some cases you will find that a certain subject area needs more material while in other cases buying fewer titles would be better since the subject is not as popular as it once was. But with a spread sheet chart for each subject it will be easy to see at a glance what is needed. You will, of course, want to use this information in combination with the other information collected. We will discuss this at greater length in the following chapters.

FIGURE 3-16 SUMMARY CHART

SUBJECT	CIRC. STATISTIC (ANNUAL)	REF/IN HOUSE USE	VOLS. OWNED	BUDGET	AGE OF COLLECTION	LEVEL NEEDED	EVALUATION OF COLL.

REFERENCES

Armstrong, Patricia. "Automated Circulation: for the Small Public Library." *Canadian Library Journal* 41 (December 1984): 334-337.

Comer, Cynthia. "List-checking as a Method for Evaluating Library Collections." *Collection Building* 3 (1981): 26-34.

Futas, Elizabeth. *The Library Forms Illustrated Handbook*. New York: Neal-Schuman Publishers, Inc., 1984.

Kohl, David. *Circulation, Interlibrary Loan, Patron Use, and Collection Maintenance: A Handbook for Library Managers*. Santa Barbara, Calif.: ABC Clio, 1986.

Osborn, Charles B. "Non-use and User Studies in Collection Development." *Collection Management* 4 (Spring-Summer 1982): 45-53.

Robbins-Carter, Jane, ed. *Public Librarianship: A Reader*. Littleton, Colo.: Libraries Unlimited, 1982.

Serebnick, Judith, ed. *Collection Management in Public Libraries*. Chicago: American Library Association, 1986.

Soltesz, David. "Automated Systems Data in the Service of Collection Development: A Public Library Experience." *Library Administration and Management* (Fall 1989): 209-212.

Zweizig, Douglas, and Dervin, Brenda. "Public Library Use, Users, Uses: Advances in Knowledge of the Characteristics and Needs of the Adult Clientele of American Public Libraries." In *Advances in Librarianship*. Edited by Melvin J. Voigt and Michael H. Harris. New York: Academic Press, 1977.

4 THE COMMUNITY

Public library collections are shaped by the needs and interests of the residents of the community. If you choose to develop a library collection in isolation or without up-to-date information about the community, your library could lack items of great interest to local users and include items of little interest. So it is necessary to survey the community and to find out more about the residents and their requirements and interests.

Many librarians assume that they can determine the needs and interests of their community by observing what materials are frequently requested and which materials circulate most. Although this is certainly one way of assessing some of the needs and interests of your patrons, it is not a comprehensive look at the community.

Materials of interest to the community must be in the collection in order to circulate; thus the information gathered at a circulation desk is only related to what the library already owns. Also, the people who come into any particular library are its present users, not its potential users. According to most surveys, on average these patrons represent only a fraction of the potential user group.

The facts collected from a survey or community analysis may reveal physical, economic, or social changes in the community that will affect the demands on your library's collection and how it is used. A community analysis is a benchmark position from which the collection development plan will be formulated and on which other library plans and changes can be based. New information from a community analysis revealed for one library that the focus of certain parts of the collection needed to be changed. Although that library was buying materials for a community with young families, in fact many residents had children in college! Another library wanted to learn why many of its patrons were using another library or purchasing the books they wanted to read. Through a survey it discovered that the collection lacked current, quality nonfiction. The collection had been geared to meet requests for best-sellers when many people wanted in-depth materials in a variety of nonfiction areas.

Information gathering on the present situation of your community is a large data-gathering process—and very important to the formulation of the library's collection development policy. A good place to start is with statistical information.

HOW TO GATHER INFORMATION

The two types of community information, statistical and nonstatistical, are gathered differently. Statistical information from the census and collecting agencies can be found in books such as the *County and City Data Book*, in pamphlets, articles, reports, and in other materials available from libraries. Statistical data can also be obtained from town, county, state, regional, and federal agencies. A good reference librarian can easily find this information, much of which is in print or electronic format.

Nonstatistical information is best gathered by questionnaires and interviews. You, your staff, volunteers, or people hired to conduct the research will either go out into the community to ask questions or survey individuals as they come into the library or questionnaires may be mailed to community residents.

STATISTICAL ANALYSIS

THE CENSUS

The United States census (produced every ten years) provides a variety of basic information about local communities. The data includes:

- the number of people living in the community,
- the number of people of each sex,
- the age of the population,
- the marital status of residents,
- races and nationalities in the community,
- languages spoken by residents,
- the occupations of the people of working age and the rate of unemployment,
- the number of children and household size,
- the educational level of residents, and
- the income of residents.

Knowing your community's population will give you an idea of the number of people the library can expect to serve. When analyzed it can be used to predict the optimal size of the collection. It is usually easy to collect this kind of data. The latest U.S. census is a good starting place. If your library does not have this data in great detail, then you'll have to locate another library near by which does have it. Large urban libraries and university libraries usually have this information particularly if they are a U.S. government documents depository.

The specific information you gather may vary slightly. Figure 4-1 is an example of a chart that arranged this information.

Here are some of the ways you can evaluate this data:

The male-female ratio in your community will help you define the collection in terms of interests related to gender. According to library studies, in traditional communities women are often interested in cooking, decorating, and creative arts projects and men are interested in sports, automobiles, and building projects. We can all think of examples of women who are more interested in cars and sports than in fashion or homemaking, but generalizations like these come from solid evidence built from many user and community surveys. You may know from the use of the library that these generalizations do not hold true in your community and will adjust your thinking accordingly. (See Carpenter, Lucas, and Soltys under References at the end of this chapter.)

The age of the population enables you to determine the number of adults, young adults, school-aged children, preschool children, and senior citizens in the community. You can tell by comparison with an earlier census what changes are taking place in the community. This data will help in the present and future development of the children's, young adult, and adult collections.

The marital status of the population, indicating whether the community has a sizable single population or if most residents are married, provides information about the lifestyle of the community's residents. It can provide some information about the kinds of library materials that might be popular based on our knowledge of the differences in reading tastes and interests of single people and married people. If the library has a large number of single people, they may have more—or less—time to read, depending on what other activities are available for them in the community, or whether the community is near a large metropolitan area or a large recreational area. Married people may have some specific library needs related to family life and children.

The different nationalities or racial groups who live in your community and—their number—will certainly have an impact on the collection. A community with a large African-American population will want works by and about African-Americans in America and in other parts of the world. Information on events in the African-American community will also be of interest. A community with a Mexican-American population may request

FIGURE 4-1 COMMUNITY INFORMATION SUMMARY

Name of Community _____

Population _____

Gender

_____ Males   _____ Females

Race

_____ White

_____ Black

_____ Hispanic

_____ Asian

_____ Other

Age

_____ under 5   _____ 5 - 14

_____ 15 - 24   _____ 25 - 34

_____ 35 - 44   _____ 45 - 54

_____ 55 - 64   _____ 65 - 74

_____ 75 and over

Education

_____ percent completing 12 years or more

_____ percent completing 16 years or more

FIGURE 4-1 *Continued*

Marital Status

_____ single

_____ married

_____ widowed

_____ divorced

Households

_____ Number of households

_____ Persons per household

_____ Female family households

_____ One person households

Income

_____ Per capita income

_____ Percent below poverty level

_____ Number of families

_____ Number of persons

Employment

_____ manufacturing

_____ retail trade

_____ finance, insurance and real estate

_____ services

_____ percent employed

_____ percent unemployed

books by authors who discuss the experiences of other members of their community in America and books written in Spanish, as well as materials to help Spanish-speaking patrons learn English.

The languages spoken in the community tells the librarian whether print and nonprint information in languages other than English are needed. For instance, there are branch libraries in New York City that have book collections in four and five languages—Spanish, Russian, Korean, Chinese, and an Indian dialect—and videos in several languages, too.

Information on the occupations of members of your community will enable you to determine if yours is a predominantly white-collar or blue-collar community, or a mix of both. Different occupational groups have different information needs. A white-collar community, for example, may want current information on investing and a large business reference collection. A blue-collar community might be best served by information on civil service exams and vocational education programs. The rate of employment indicates whether the library is in a community with some hidden or not-so-hidden economic problems. Those seeking employment might be well served by a job information center with information on resumes, interviewing skills and new career options.

Knowing the number of children and their ages, as well as the number of households, in your community will help the library gear its children's collection more accurately to the needs of the community. For instance, the sudden increase in births we're currently experiencing means that many children have older parents. These parents, many of whom have postponed parenthood until their careers were in place, may understand the value of reading to their children and so use the library more. They'll demand large book and nonprint collections and children's programs along with parenting collections.

Data on the level of education provides at least an indication of the level of materials which may be requested by the community. For example, a population in which many hold graduate degrees may make requests for university press books and materials on more advanced levels. You cannot, however, assume that lower educational levels mean less sophisticated tastes.

With income data an analysis can be made of how people with different levels of income use the library and what they read. For example, a high-income community might be more interested in books on travel and computers while a low-income community might be more interested in do-it-yourself manuals or adult independent learner projects.

OTHER STATISTICAL DATA

Census data should be analyzed in combination with other statistical information about the community. In one library, an analysis of education level and income level revealed an educated population working in the service professions (teaching and social work where salaries are low) and making great demands on the library (see Bob, Chatham, and Wood under Reference at the end of this chapter). Another library compared population figures with library registration figures to determine what portion of the community the library was serving. The registration figures indicated that only 10 percent of the potential users actually had library cards and borrowed material from the library. As a result, it was determined that the library should mount a registration drive to increase enrollment and encourage greater use of the library, targeting to those judged most likely to become active users.

State, county, regional, and local governments issue reports and do statistical surveys far more frequently than the U.S. census. Their results are more up-to-date and thus more appropriate to use for current acquisitions of materials and for developing a collection development policy. These data include business statistics and a more current look at income, education levels, household size, age, and racial and national mix.

Often ignored by governmental statistical sources, but sometimes picked up by local groups who do their own surveying, are current statistics on special populations. For instance, data on the disabled and homebound may be available from a local social service agency. The best statistics on senior citizens are probably available from local departments for the aging or groups that help provide social security or medicaid benefits to those over 65 years of age. School districts do their own surveys to gather accurate information on the school-aged population in the community. Other organizations that may be a source of data include the American Association of University Women, the League of Women Voters, and the Chamber of Commerce. Local chambers of commerce will have information on local business and industry which can be invaluable. A local arts organization will have information on such cultural institutions as community theaters, art galleries and museums. They will also know about crafts people, artists and performing arts groups in the community. It is important to look for such surveys on a regular basis to glean more information about the community.

NONSTATISTICAL COMMUNITY INFORMATION

The current interests of the community are an important factor in collection development. These interests may be related to work, school, independent study, or educational and cultural interests. It is important to get a feel for the community—its values and beliefs; its tensions and conflicts; the emphasis it places on its institutions such as schools, churches, government—and the library; the ways in which community problems are mediated, and what forces work for and against community change. These interests can be identified in various ways. Certainly local newspapers, radio, and television provide a great deal of information. A local, radio talk show is a wonderful place to get information about what some people in the community think about current issues. Newsletters from local groups also provide a great deal of information, as do publications that are issued from town and county governments.

There usually are members of a community who, as a result of their positions of power, are a good source of information. These gatekeepers can range from the local storekeeper, or retired teacher, or a law enforcement person to the mayor's or school principal's spouse. You should try to identify these people and recruit them for your team. The information that is gathered about the library's collection and its circulation patterns combined with the information from individual community members will guide you in deciding what kinds, levels, and formats of material the library should supply to its reading public.

SURVEYING THE COMMUNITY

There are a number of ways the library can collect information on the community and the library's users. The best is the community survey. Through the community survey the library can evaluate the effectiveness of the collection and related services, get information on specific community problems, identify user groups in need of service and identify new trends in the community.

You can use a variety of techniques for your community survey:

- Volunteers can go house to house and ask people to fill out the questionnaire or conduct an interview.
- The questionnaire can be sent in the mail either separately or as part of a community-wide newsletter.
- Or, interviews can be done by phone.

Since no survey is perfect, you must decide which will work best for you and which will be most appropriate. You may wish you could do a house to house survey but know that this is simply not feasible in your community. You may decide to include a survey in the library's newsletter which is mailed to each resident realizing that you may have a low response. You may want to combine two or more methods—a survey included in the library newsletter with a telephone survey which will sample the community. In any case you will need to evaluate the time and money you have to expend on this endeavor knowing that the house to house survey will be the most expensive and time consuming and a mail survey the least. Often an outside consultant is useful to help you decide which method to use.

QUESTIONNAIRES

In deciding to collect information on a community, the format of the survey tool must be designed. If it is to be a questionnaire, what is it to look like, who is to receive it, who is to administer it, and who is to analyze its data must all be decided beforehand. If it is to be an interview of users, nonusers, or all residents, you must devise questions ahead of time. Neither questions in print nor verbal interviews are easy to do. Time must be spent on pretesting, so that errors are not made. Long after a set of questionnaires had been devised, one library found out that the day on which it had decided to give out the questionnaire, excluded an entire group of users. The day, a Wednesday, was chosen because it is a busy day since materials were due back. Unfortunately, a certain group of patrons was excluded because they rarely showed up on that day. It seems that the circulation clerk knew that the very large women's garden club met elsewhere on Wednesday. These patrons were, therefore, systematically excluded from the questionnaire survey. Always ask the support staff for advice on the best time to interview or distribute the questionnaires.

In-house surveys can provide a wealth of information on the ideas and interests of those community residents who use the

FIGURE 4-2 QUESTIONNAIRE

The MMPL is trying to improve its collections and services to you. We hope you will take a few minutes to fill out this form and return it to us.

_____ Male   _____ Female

AGE:

Age at last birthday _____

EDUCATION:

What is the last year of school you completed?

_____ K - 6   _____ Some high school   _____ High school graduate

_____ Two year college/technical school graduate   _____ Some college

_____ Four year college graduate   _____ Masters degree

_____ Doctorate   _____ Professional degree (please specify)

INCOME:

What is your total family income?

_____ Under $10,000   _____ $10,000 - $19,000

_____ $20,000 - $29,999   _____ $30,000 - $39,999

_____ $40,000 - $49,000   _____ $50,000 - $59,999

_____ $60,000 - $75,000   _____ over $75,000

RESIDENCE:

Where do you live?

    (list parts of your community and adjoining areas)

    _____ Own   _____ Rent

FIGURE 4-2 *Continued*

EMPLOYMENT:

Where do you work?

____ Manufacturing   ____ Transportation and communications

____ Professional services   ____ Wholesale and retail sales

____ Entertainment and recreation services   ____ Farming

____ Finance, insurance and realestate

____ Personal services (including working in the home)

THE LIBRARY:

When did you last visit the library?

____ within the last week   ____ within 14 days

____ last month   ____ last year

____ more often   ____ less often   ____ never

If you did visit the library, what was the purpose of your visit?

____ find something to read   ____ find information for a project

____ go to a program   ____ adult   ____ children's

____ borrow audiovisual material   ____ video   ____ audiocassette

____ Other (please explain)

Did you find what you needed?

____ yes   ____ no   ____ partially successful

Any suggestions you would like to make to any of us on the

library staff._____

_____

Thank you for your help on this survey.

FIGURE 4-3 COMMUNITY ORGANIZATION FORM

Name of Organization _____

Address_____

Telephone Number (s) _____

Officers:

    President _____

    Vice President _____

    Program Chair _____

Please check major areas of interest for your organization

_____ Business

_____ Arts/Culture

_____ Education

_____ Health

_____ Politics & Government

_____ Recreation

_____ Professional

_____ Service

_____ Other

FIGURE 4-3 *Continued*

What age groups does your organization include and/or serve?

_____ Children (up to age 12)

_____ Young Adults (ages 13 - 18)

_____ Adults (19 - 60)

_____ Older Adults (over 60)

Are you part of a national or international organization?

_____ yes   _____ no

What library services does your organization need?

_____ Reading lists

_____ Exhibits

_____ List of speakers for meetings

_____ Use of meeting room

_____ Information on reference service

_____ Information on services for the handicapped

_____ Loan of audiovisual equipment

_____ Workshop on program planning

_____ Workshop on discussion-group leadership

library. These are the people most interested in the library; so it's important that you know as much about them as possible. We know from national polls that approximately one-third of the country's population uses the library. This third of the population tends to be middle-class. In recent years, many libraries have begun to deal almost exclusively with patrons who use the library in order to raise circulation and fund other programs. Their efforts involve giving these people more of what they want in order to raise library use figures, which in turn may raise budgets, which can be used to start new programs. The backbone of any library is its users, so a good place to start is with them. Sampling is usually the best way to do this. You can develop a short questionnaire which can be filled out in no more than ten minutes. Usually the library will use volunteers or perhaps pages and clerical staff who will greet people at the door and ask them to take a few minutes to fill out the questionnaire. You'll want to plan to do the survey at different times of the day and on different days of the week to get as wide a sampling as possible. Another more elaborate way to do an in-house survey is to have volunteers or paid personnel actually interview people about their use of the library. This is, of course, much more time consuming and expensive but provides you with more detailed information.

In developing a questionnaire or questions for an interview you may want to seek some professional advice from someone in a sociology or psychology department or from a marketing concern. In any case you should keep in mind the following:

- decide what information you want to get from the questionnaire or interview;
- plan in advance how you are going to tabulate your material so that you can see if the questions you have framed will produce the results you want;
- ask questions that can be answered "yes" or "no" plus an optional "undecided," "don't know," or "other";
- leave more time for tabulating the results if you plan to ask open-ended questions;
- use simple language, neutral in tone;
- test the time it takes to complete the questionnaire;
- pretest your questionnaire with a small group to discover any problems such as questions that can't be answered;
- enclose a cover letter and a stamped, self-addressed envelope if you use a questionnaire.

You should know that a 20 percent response is a good return on a questionnaire which must be mailed back. Another interesting fact that may influence your decision on whether to use a questionnaire or an interview is the opinion of some experts that an interview can be longer than a quesionnaire.

In Figure 4-2 is a list of sample questions for a questionnaire.

Once the data has been gathered, it will need to be compiled and evaluated. Although this may seem to be a simple project, it can be fairly complex if you are to get as much information as possible from the data. You may want to hire someone to help you with this part of the process if you have no one on your staff with expertise in this area. With this information you will be able to compile a better picture of your users and how they use the library as well as a picture of nonusers.

COMMUNITY ORGANIZATIONS

A great deal of information can be collected through community organizations. You should attend as many community meetings as possible and develop contacts with major groups to keep current on their activities. In fact, contact all local organizations at least once a year in order to update the library's information on them— their officers, current projects and programs, and any special events they are planning. Develop a survey form such as in Figure 4-3 so that you will collect your information in a uniform manner.

Community organizations will indicate areas in which the library must be able to meet community needs and interests on a group basis. Responding to the needs of organizations means the library can reach a large number of people in the community in a more organized fashion. In analyzing the reponses to your questionnaire the library may find out more about the groups in its community. Some of the groups the library may serve are the following:

- Parents and teachers who are active in groups like PTAs and who are interested in materials that supplement assignments given to their children in the classroom and who want to better understand the teaching methods being used, such as the whole language method of teaching reading.
- Hobby groups that want information about their hobby. Hobbyists sometimes form clubs; for example, a group of people who hike decided to start a hiking club. People in this club are interested in

materials on hiking and on interesting areas to which they can plan trips.

- Political clubs (the Democrats and Republicans and their subgroups for women and youth) and groups that have an interest in the political process—for example, the League of Women Voters, which uses the public library as a site for nonpartisan political discussions and debates. The League of Women Voters particularly is a group that uses the library heavily. They study topics, which include the courts, environmental issues, housing, issues pertaining to voting or issues involving local government.
- Chamber of Commerce as well as merchant groups and other business networking groups that need information from the library's business reference collection.
- Service clubs including the Lions, Kiwanis, Exchange, Zonta, Soroptimist, and Altrusa. These groups of business and professional people need information for home and work.
- Health-related organizations such as the Red Cross, heart association, cancer association, visiting nurses, and others dealing with specific diseases or dealing with more general health problems will use the library to document and research current information sources.
- The historical association and related groups such as the Daughters of the American Revolution (DAR) are always library users. They want historical and genealogical materials on the community and its residents.
- Youth groups in the community which includes the Scouts, Camp Fire Girls, 4H, Big Brother and Big Sister, and other girls and boys clubs. These groups want to visit the library to hear book talks and to view films. They may also have special projects that involve the library.

LOCAL GOVERNMENT

The politics of the local community can be very important in understanding how things work and who makes the decisions. Each local government has its own personality, which often changes with an election. Much of what happens in a community is affected by what goes on at the local level. Find out as much as you can— the type of government (mayor-council, council-manager, etc.), what departments there are (sanitation, fire, water, parks and recreation, etc.), what function the local government performs, what the issues are that are being dealt with by local government, how it is changing, and what new functions are being added. Get an organizational chart so you can see who reports to whom and how the hierarchy works. With this information you will be better able to evaluate the potential information needs of your local government.

BUSINESS COMMUNITY

The climate of the business community also affects the library. The library will want to keep up-to-date on what is happening with local businesses and whether the economic climate in the community is a healthy one. The health of the business community, of course, affects employment and the economic level of local residents. It is also useful to know what kinds of businesses exist in the community—the number of factories and manufacturing establishments, institutions that employ people such as local government, hospitals, retail stores, service stores such as restaurants and shoe repairs, and professional people such as physicians and lawyers. This may indicate the interests of the community as much as any survey can. Look at the economic base of the community and what industries and businesses predominate. You'll begin to understand what changes in the national economy will most affect your community.

The number of movie houses, video stores, and record and disk stores may indicate a trend in the type of recreation that interests many people of the community. It might be wise, if a number of businesses close for the season, to determine the size and interests of the summer population.

Not all information on the community can be gathered from printed data. Some must be gathered from the citizens themselves. The best way to do this is to get to know the community—to stay in contact with both groups and individuals in the business sector. The best information sources, however, are the individuals you meet at their place of business, in the library, in the street, in the grocery store, or even on the movie line. Stop and talk to people. This is one of the best ways to gather newsworthy information. It is a time consuming but rewarding part of a librarian's job.

ENVIRONMENT

Whether a community is fairly isolated or a suburb of a big city will affect how your library's collection is used. A library in a town isolated by mountains may be the only cultural resource for hundreds of miles and so will be used by residents for most of their reading, research, recreational, educational, and work-related needs. People living near a big city may use different libraries—a library at their workplace, a college library which is convenient and open to the general public, and the public library. You need to assess your own situation and document how it affects the use of

GET A FEEL FOR THE COMMUNITY:
—its values and beliefs,
—its tensions and conflicts,
—the emphasis it places on its institutions,
—the ways community problems are mediated,
—what forces work for and against community change.

your library and thus of your collection. You will want to add questions to your surveys and interviews to ask what other libraries are used, and whether your patrons participate in other cultural events, or whether they depend heavily on this particular library.

A library can be affected by the general climatological region in which it is located. A cold-weather climate may induce people to borrow a large number of books at a time, since they spend a great deal of time indoors; a climate which is warm all year round will bring patrons to use the library during the hottest times when their outdoor activities are restricted. Public libraries in a warm climate may promote programs with an emphasis on sports that can be played in the community all year round, e.g., soccer. Or it may emphasize programs on nature-appreciation, which can be enjoyed in all seasons, i.e., identification of trees and shrubs; and other programs which include book discussions. Since retired persons tend to pick these areas to settle in, the climate might indicate that the library look more closely at the age of its clientele and develop its programming and collections accordingly. A cold climate, on the other hand, may require a more liberal loan period to escape the necessities of weather-related fines on materials. Programs and materials on sports for a colder climate might be appropriate, for example, skiing, tobogganing, sledding, curling, etc. or ideas for indoor projects. Although this is harder to quantify, your impressions as to how climatic conditions affect the library are still an important consideration.

SMALL GROUPS AND INDIVIDUAL USERS
Every community consists of a broad spectrum of individuals whose interests can affect materials collected in its library. If there are politically active people in the area, materials related to their activities, such as on how to run a political campaign, become very important. People interested in the education system will want current materials on new educational methods.

Some individuals stand out from a group of users because of the uniqueness of their claim on the library's resources and materials—for example, individuals who request special formats (talking books for the blind, telephone capability for the deaf), and individuals who request special services (shut-in service or nursing home visits). These needs should be documented so you can evaluate the level of use and of need. Add the statistics on these services to the data you are collecting.

Knowing that there are groups and individuals with specific needs will help you to serve them better by selecting the proper material. You can document these needs through your work with community groups. For example, one library built a specialized collection as a result of the death of a child by a drunk driver. The community was galvanized into creating a MADD (Mothers Against Drunk Driving) group. The library responded by buying books on lobbying government officials and on organizing and running a local advocacy group.

In another community the librarian was working with a group that was interested in local history. It wanted to research the history of the area and arrange celebrations to commemorate certain historical events. The town was planning to celebrate the 250th birthday of its founding. A great deal of information on its origins was found by using historical documents found in the library. In researching the library's local history collection it was discovered that the town was linked with a major effort in the state, not recognized at the time as something important, but recognized in retrospect as an event worth commemorating.

In another case, members of a community theater group used the library as a resource to do the research for fundraising by examining the library's guides to foundations and granting agencies. They also did a great deal of research on how to organize and successfully run an arts organization.

People raising families have need of all kinds of materials to help them with their young children—they may want to know more about toilet training or how to help a child who is having difficulty in school. They may have an impact on the number of picture books in the children's section or the number of psychology books in the adult nonfiction section. Your study of the census data may have already prepared you for this group.

It will assist you in analyzing your information if you put it in a chart. Figure 4-4 shows a chart that can be used to summarize the information you have collected on your community's activities and interests.

EDUCATIONAL RESOURCES

The library will want to pay special attention to educational and library facilities within the community. They have a particularly important relationship to the library, so it is necessary to survey what exists. There may be public schools, private schools, religious

FIGURE 4-4 COMMUNITY ACTIVITIES AND INTERESTS

ACTIVITIES & INTERESTS	PRIMARY	SECONDARY	TERTIARY
Politics & Government			
Religion			
Business			
Education			
Sports			
Culture			
Environmental Issues			
Health Issues			
Community Service			
Other			

EXPLANATION: You can use this chart to describe the activities and interests of your community. You may want to change the categories or add more categories to more accurately describe your community. This is simply a visual way of summarizing the information you have gathered.

schools, vocational schools, adult education and continuing education courses, and perhaps some schools of higher education, such as a community or junior college or even a four-year college or university. These all have an impact on the use of the library and its collections. It is important to find out through discussions with them what they expect of their students and how they expect them to fulfill course requirements. It is possible that these discussions may add to your understanding of the community.

SCHOOL MEDIA CENTER RESOURCES

The local public schools have libraries. What kind of resources do these libraries have—the size of the collections and the formats available? Do they have cooperative arrangements with other institutions. Do they have an automated circulation system or an online catalog? Explore what resources can be shared. Can a delivery service be arranged between the two or more libraries involved; can public library patrons use the school libraries on-site, can the public library borrow collections of books or audio-visual materials from the school collections during the summer?

ACADEMIC LIBRARY RESOURCES

There may be a university, college, or community college nearby with a sizable library collection. Find out about the size of the collection, the formats purchased and the automation which has been done. Find out if the academic institution allows outsiders to use its materials on-site. It may allow certain of its resources to be used but not others. Or it may allow for on-site use but not borrowing. In any case a community is always extremely lucky to have an institution of higher learning nearby.

OTHER EDUCATIONAL RESOURCES

There will be other educational institutions in the community which may be hidden resources. They may have limited collections and may have very specific rules about the use of their materials, but at a minimum they will be a good source for difficult reference questions and at best they will allow the public library to send patrons over to use their facilities. Some examples of these special institutional collections in the community might be at the local art museum, town hall, local businesses or companies, or the local historical society.

REGIONAL LIBRARY RESOURCES

Library networks, cooperatives, and consortiums will be of great value in sharing resources and helping the public library to supply the needs of its more sophisticated users. Networks vary considerably depending on the part of the country. Some are state legislated and include nearly all the libraries in the state. In other cases, libraries may have formed their own cooperatives and consortiums to do resource sharing and to share a variety of other services such as technical services.

It is important to find out what exists in your area. It can mean that the library will not have to develop in-depth collections in subjects for which it has little demand and will enable it to build better collections in the most used parts of its collection.

Balancing access to other materials with the library's own collection is a tricky act. The library must weigh the advantage of having materials accessible on-site versus making patrons wait. These determinations will have to be made on a subject-by-subject basis so they reflect the patron's need for immediate access, the speed of delivery from other sites, and the kind of relationship the library is attempting to develop with its community.

SUMMARY

You have no doubt collected a great deal of information about your community which you can use in developing both the library's collection and its collection development plan. Two charts will summarize much of this information—the community profile and community activities and interests. Other data will be derived from the community surveys you have done. As you write your collection development policy, you will use this data to explain your decisions.

REFERENCES

Bob, Murray L. "Library Use, Reading, and the Economy." *Library Journal* 110 (February 15, 1985): 105-107.

Bone, Larry Earl, ed. "Community Analysis and Libraries." *Library Trends* 24 (January 1976): 429-643.

Carpenter, Ray L. "The Public Library Patron." *Library Journal* 104 (February 1, 1979): 348.

Chatman, Elfreda A. "Low Income and Leisure: Implications for Public Library Use." *Public Libraries* 24 (Spring 1985): 34-36.

Daniel, Wayne W. *Questionnaire Design: a Selected Bibliography for the Survey Researcher.* Monticello: Vance, 1979.

Kim, Choong Han, and Little, Robert David. *Public Library Users and Uses; A Market Research Handbook*. Metuchen, N.J.: Scarecrow, 1987.

Line, Maurice. *Library Surveys: An Introduction to Their Use, Planning, Procedure and Presentation*. 2nd ed. Revised by Sue Stone. London: Bingley Books, 1982.

Lucas, Linda. "Life Style, Reading, and Library Use." *Public Libraries* 18 (Spring 1979): 22.

Martin, Allie Beth. "Studying the Community: an Overview." *Library Trends* 24 (January 1976):483-496.

Monroe, Margaret E. "Community Development as a Mode of Community Analysis." *Library Trends* 24 (January 1976): 497-514.

Oppenheimer, A. N. *Questionnaire Design and Attitude Measurement*. New York: Basic Books, 1966.

Output Measures for Public Libraries: A Manual of Standardized Procedures. 2nd edition. Prepared for the Public Library Development Project by Nancy A. Van House, et al. Chicago: American Library Association, 1987.

Payne, Stanley L. *The Art of Asking Questions*. Princeton: Princeton University Press, 1951.

Planning & Role Setting for Public Libraries: A Manual of Options and Procedures. 2nd edition. Prepared for the Public Library Development Project by Charles R. McClure et al. Chicago: American Library Association, 1987.

Soltys, Amy. "Planning and Implementing a Community Survey." *Canadian Library Journal* 42 (October 1985): 245-249.

Warncke, Ruth. *Studying the Community*. Chicago: American Library Association, 1960.

Warren, R.L *Studying Your Community*. New York: Russell Sage Foundation, 1955.

Wood, Leonard. "The Gallup Survey: Library Use: An Irregular Habit." *Publishers Weekly* 228 (November 22, 1985): 20-21.

5 THE COLLECTION DEVELOPMENT POLICY

The collection development policy is used to introduce present and future board members, staff, community groups, and others to your library's policies and procedures. It provides the basis for the systematic development of the library's collection. The process through which it is developed is one of its most important strengths. If it is developed by a group that represents many parts of the community and is based on the information collected about the library and the community, it will have strong supporters who will carry the word about the library to all parts of the community. It will provide the community with a better understanding of the library and library staff with more interaction with its community. Its public relations value is enormous.

Basically, the collection development policy contains most of the following sections:

1. Mission, goals, objectives
2. Community analysis
3. Materials selection
4. Maintenance
5. Evaluation
6. Special collections
7. Networks, consortiums, cooperation
8. Intellectual freedom, censorship, the law

Some libraries will have only some of the sections in their policy statements, most will have all of them and some will have added others based on their own needs and interests. Some policy statements will be written out in very specific terms, most will generalize in order not to date the policy and thus necessitate annual revisions. Some libraries will state the policy, most will try to explain it as it relates to the readers of the document.

MISSION, GOALS STATEMENT, AND OBJECTIVES

The mission of the library as an institution should be a very general statement of the value of a library to its community. It should be only a paragraph or two and be capable of being followed with few changes for some time, preferably a decade. Many collection development policies start with a statement of purpose. Here is one example: "It is our mission to be freely available to our citizens in the area of their informational needs." If a mission statment is not available, these policies are often introduced by the library's goals statement—the purpose of the library. You should appoint a subcommittee of the collection development committee to review and/or develop such a statement based on the information gathered about the library and the community. They should try to write a statement that not only outlines broad goals for the library but highlights some specifics. It should accurately reflect the library's present situation and priorities and set goals for future development. For example, the statement might reflect the fact that the library considers its support of the informational needs of local government, business, and community organizations and associations one of its most important goals. You will want your goals statement to cover:

1. How the library relates to the formal and informal education structure in the community.

   This will differ greatly from community to community. The formal education structure may not only comprise public schools; it may include a two- or four-year college. The informal structure could include adult basic education programs, continuing education programs, historical associations, private or corporate collections, and a host of other information agencies available in varying degrees to the community. Whatever these education structures are, the goals statement will want to include an area of cooperation, networking, consortium, or other cooperative elements in the nature of educational institutions as a whole. The library's reliance on the availability of resources in these other institutions should be noted in some general way in a goals statement, indicate that this has been done so that the most effective use of tax monies can be made.

2. How the library relates to governmental units, community organizations, and groups of local residents with similar interests or needs.

   This might include a special goal the library has, for instance, serving the physically handicapped, new Americans, or new adult readers.

3. How the library supports individual needs—informational needs, general educational needs, recreational needs, the need for intellectual growth, etc.

   In this area, a goal would be the fulfillment of individual growth. Stated in goals terminology it might read like this: The library sees as one of its primary goals the support of individuals trying to educate themselves as they take up their roles as educated citizenry in order to uphold the democratic way of life. For a person to vote intelligently, the issues must be known. Thus one of the overarching goals of most libraries is to provide the kinds of collections that will allow for this self-education.

4. How the library will respond to the changing needs and the new interests of the residents of the community.

   It's important that your goals statement indicate that the library wants and intends to respond to the future, as well as the past and the present.

5. What role the library plans to play in promoting reading and introducing print, audiovisual resources, and information technology to the community.

   In stating the importance of literacy, of sources of information in all formats, and of the newer technologies that serve your public, you will want to have at least one goal statement that defines the library's role in providing these resources to the community.

Your goals statement should be reviewed and revised every five years to keep up with changes in the library and the community. As in all processes, the time period for review differs with the extent of the changes in the community, which must be reflected in the changes in the goals of the institutions which serve that community. The fewer changes that take place, the longer the established goals will prevail. When the statement does need revising, however, it should be done using the same process that has been suggested to create the original statement.

The objectives of the library are more specific than the goals—they describe how the goals will be met. The objectives follow your goals and provide more specific information about each stated goal. If, for example, your goal is "to meet the informational needs of the entire community," then the objective might be "to respond to all requests for information and to build an in-depth reference collection in areas of new and continuing interest to the community." If one of your goals is to "enhance job-related knowledge and skills," then the objective might be "to build a special job information section in the library."

THE COMMUNITY TO BE SERVED

Include a brief description in the collection development policy of the community your library serves. It can cover the population, schools, businesses, geographic location, the residents by age (preschoolers, elementary school students, junior and senior high school students, adults and senior citizens), professions (teachers, small business owners, service professionals, blue collar workers, government employees, etc.), interest areas (education, local government, recreation, etc.), and special characteristics (foreign born, new adult readers, handicapped users). All this information will be readily available as a result of the information gathered during the planning process.

An optional approach is to give a brief, general description of the community and emphasize the changes occurring. You might, for example, discuss the closing of a company by a major employer that has forced many local residents to find other employment, or move to other communities.

MATERIALS SELECTION

The core part of the collection development policy concerns materials selection. From the survey of the library's collection and the ensuing evaluation you'll have good documentation on the present status of the library's collection—its strengths and weaknesses—as well as information about the community's needs and interests.

PURPOSE
The section on materials selection starts with an overall philosophical statement about the aim of the library's collection to meet the needs, stated and unstated, of the majority of local residents.

For example, a small public library would no doubt state that it aims "to provide current, popular material"; not that "it does not attempt to collect scholarly material, rare books, or manuscripts." Discussion of special selection goals for different age groups and other special groups should be covered in a section on selection by clientele. Information on obtaining materials not in the library's collection can be covered in the network section.

LEGAL RESPONSIBILITY

You'll want to clarify the legal responsibilities for selection, state how these responsibilities are delegated, and the selection procedures. Provide a general description of how selections are made, who is involved, how decisions are reached, and who is responsible for the selection decisions. This will indicate that the board of trustees is legally responsible for all decisions, but that the Director or the Head of Collection Development has been delegated the day-to-day responsibility for selection decisions. A brief description of the selection process will no doubt be useful to the public. For example, explain that materials are purchased based on reviews or that all decisions are made by a library selection committee. It could also indicate how the library deals with suggestions from the community.

CRITERIA

The materials selection section should list the criteria for selection. It might include statements on the following points for print, nonfiction works:

1. The need for material that is accurate and up-to-date. This is particularly crucial in rapidly changing subject areas such as medicine, investment and finance, or computers.
2. The need for material that provides an informative point of view.
3. The importance of evaluating the reputation and authority of authors and publishers.
4. The selection of material that is readable and comprehensible to its intended audience. Sometimes an excellent book on a subject is simply too scholarly for a lay audience, and the librarian must search for a more appropriate work in that area.
5. The need for good technical quality in printing, binding, illustrations, and design. For example, a book

that has very small print and not enough white space on a page can be hard to read.

6. The need to evaluate the book in relation to its price. If a book is terribly expensive, the library may want to wait for a more reasonably priced book on the subject.
7. The need for materials on topics of high interest or emerging issues.
8. The contribution that a work makes to its subject area. If a work is without equal in a subject area, you may want to purchase it even if it does not meet the other criteria.
9. The level of indexing which increases or decreases the usefulness of a book.

For fiction, the criteria might include some of the above, plus:

1. Plausible plot and good plot development.
2. Effective characterization.
3. Imaginative writing and originality.
4. Appropriate level for the age for which it is intended.
5. Literary merit.
6. Accurate descriptions of the particular era or country in which it is set.
7. Ability to sustain the reader's interest.
8. Significant contributions in a new or special way if a new edition.

For nonprint materials, the criteria parallel most of those listed for print materials but should also include statements on technical quality with descriptions of what technical excellence comprises and the appropriateness of the media chosen:

1. Artistic merit and reputation of the artist(s).
2. Quality of interpretation and technique of the artist(s).
3. Ability to be easily understood and articulated in an interesting manner, if spoken word.
4. Presentation of quality images, color representation, composition, if visual media.

FORMAT

The format of materials purchased is an important consideration. Format may include paperbacks, periodicals, pamphlets, newspapers, documents, microforms, maps, audiovisual materials, and computer software. Often collection development policies deal with each format that the library collects in a brief paragraph or two, including specific criteria for choosing that format and some special reviewing tools used. For example, the library may state that it purchases only videocassettes, audiocassettes, and computer software noting special guidelines for special formats. It may be necessary to have a separate section on audiovisual selection with its own criteria, selection process, etc. A selection policy for audiocassettes might include the following criteria:

1. The need for good technical quality.
2. The artistic merit and reputation of the artist(s).
3. The quality of interpretation and the technique of the artist(s).
4. Easy to understand and interestingly read or recited, if spoken word.

A selection policy for videos might include the following criteria:

1. The need to balance popular demand with quality which is done by basing all purchases on reviews.
2. The need for good technical quality.
3. The need for nonfiction and documentary to present accurate and up-to-date information.
4. The need for the subject to be appropriate to the video format.

A selection policy for computer software might include the following:

1. The need for good documentation that is also easy to understand.
2. The need for user friendly software.
3. The need for the program to have a large enough capacity to hold and process as many records as needed.
4. The need for good vendor support.

In addition to the criteria, different for each format, there may be inclusions and exclusions pertinent to only that particular format. In the example of the audio cassettes, you might say that only spoken word audio cassettes in English will be purchased.

MATERIALS NOT PURCHASED

It is important to discuss the kinds of materials which are not purchased. Include a list of what the library does not buy; the public may wonder why certain items are not in the collection. This list may include specific formats, such as slides or 16mm films, or types of material, such as synopses, abridged works, workbooks, outlines, or books in only certain languages.

REVIEW SOURCES

Some libraries include a list of review sources used for selection (placed in the appendix for easy revision) or a general statement on the kinds of review sources used, such as standard library periodicals and specialized works in the field.

LEVELS OF SELECTION

Definitions of the various levels of selection belong in the written collection development policy because they make selection decisions more understandable to the people for whom the policy is written. There can be any number of levels of selection, since they are created and defined by those who create the policy. We have devised the following four levels:

1. Popular or recreational level: The library buys current titles from lists of best-sellers or from experience of what titles are likely to be best sellers or important books on the "hot" topics of the day.
2. General information level: The library buys a large number of current titles and a limited number of retrospective titles on topics of interest to the clientele served.
3. Instructional level: The library buys many of the current titles available on the subject, which are not scholarly, and has or will purchase a wide assortment of retrospective titles.
4. Reference level: The library buys as many of the current titles, which are not scholarly, as possible and as wide an assortment of retrospective titles as its budget allows.

You'll want to state what the level of selection is for each major subject area. For example, contemporary music may be developed at a popular level because there is a limited demand for it; political science will be developed at an instructional level if many adults and students continually request this material; and European travel will be developed at a general information level because only current titles are of interest to the users of this section. These levels will be determined by the information gathered on use, circulation data, and interests of the community. Collection on certain levels of certain subjects will, of course, be adjusted as the interests and needs of the community change. You might want to do as they have done in the *Collection Development Plan for the Skokie Public Library (IL)*: For each subject area they stated the past collection development level, the current collection selection level and the future collection development level.

SELECTION BY SUBJECT

Many library collection policies discuss each subject area in order to describe in some detail how the Library plans to develop that particular subject. An example of this from the *Collection Development Plan of the Skokie Public Library (IL)* is on page 96.

SELECTION BY CLIENTELE

Policies developed for specialized groups often cover special materials acquired for this clientele; the relationship of other educational resources to this group, like school media centers and their curriculum materials; and the appropriateness of particular materials for them. If there are significant numbers of easily defined groups, policies should be formulated for them. For instance, if there is a sizable population of people with physical handicaps, it would be important to define how the library handles requests for talking books or books in braille.

Many library policies discuss selection by age, which is useful since it can define some of the special needs and interests of a particular age group. The most common age groups discussed in a collection development policy are children and young adults. This can be done in general terms, i.e. how selection for these two groups differs from that of other groups, or it can replicate the adult selection policy outlining the criteria for fiction and nonfiction and areas of emphasis. Special goals for the collections may be defined, such as bringing the best of children's literature to the children of the community, providing materials for children's enjoyment and enrichment, and supplementing but not duplicating the resources of the school media center. In a large urban area, the library may want to define how it will serve populations that speak languages other than English.

SUBJECT: Biography

Description: The biography collection consists of factual materials about people from all walks of life, all nationalities, and from ancient times to the present. Autobiographies, memoirs, and volumes of correspondence are also included in the collection. Many of the titles are translations from foreign languages. To support the North Suburban Library System Coordinated Acquisitions Program (CAP) in American and English Literature, the Library acquires numerous biographies of literary figures.

Influencing Factors: A well-informed community has a strong interest in reading about the lives of influential and/or interesting people. The materials are used by those pursuing independent study and by casual browsers. High school and college students from Skokie and the surrounding communities use the biography collection for their assignments.

Selection Plan: Besides the standard selection tools, reviewing sources such as *Wilson Library Bulletin* are looked at regularly. One to three copies of a title are ordered depending on patron demand. Hardcover editions are preferred over paperbacks.

Retention and Weeding: Retention of titles is based on the biographee having enduring importance. Poorly written biographies of important people are replaced by new quality titles. Popular works about people of current interest are withdrawn as soon as interest has ceased. Because of the CAP collection, literary biographies are weeded judiciously. Sources such as *Public Library Catalog, Books in Print, Readers Advisor,* and *People in Books* may be consulted before a title is withdrawn. Weeding of extra copies, books in poor condition, and ephemeral works must be done yearly. Within a three year cycle a complete reexamination of materials that are infrequently used must be done in order to maintain space for new books.

Development Plan: The biography collection is very comprehensive so little retrospective development is required. New works need to be purchased to keep up with popular demand and to maintain a well-balanced and wide-ranging section. Replacement of worn out or missing titles is ongoing. This is an area which will have a moderate reduction in size.

REPLACEMENTS

The replacement issue is an important one since many patrons expect the library to replace titles that contain dated material and titles on subjects for which better materials are available. You'll want to cover what the library's policy is on replacement. Does it replace any book in print which has been lost or damaged beyond repair? Does it replace out-of-print titles?

Guidelines for replacements might include the following points:

1. The number of copies available. If a copy is lost or missing, the library may not replace it if it owns another copy.
2. The coverage the library has on the subject. If the library has a large collection of materials in a particular subject area, there may be no reason to replace a particular title.
3. The amount of similar material available. If lots of books are continually published on a subject, the library may replace a missing title with something more current.
4. The demand for material in that subject area. It may be that a subject is so popular that the library will replace it at once.
5. The availability of the particular title. If a title is out-of-print and expensive to replace, the library will not purchase a new one.

DUPLICATES

What is the library's policy on buying duplicates? Is it based on the number of reserves or does some quality judgment go into the decision? Do you use a rental collection to supplement books you purchase? Library users are usually impatient to get materials so they should know if the number of reserves influences the number of copies that a library purchases. The library also needs a policy that addresses the duplicating of popular titles but not providing multiple copies to meet school assignments.

NEW FORMATS

It is wise to spell out the decision-making process on new formats so that patrons understand why a particular format is not available or not yet available. It may be that the format is too fragile for the library or that the equipment for it is not widely available.

GIFTS

Gift materials are yet another part of materials selection. Although you do not necessarily choose them, gifts can be a source of rare, unusual, or expensive items, as well as items for which the library has no use for a variety of reasons. The collection development policy must state that the library is free to decide whether all or part of a gift is to be kept or disposed of elsewhere. The gift policy should include the following:

1. Criteria for evaluating gifts.
2. Criteria for formats other than books. For example, if the library receives a gift periodical subscription, will it be treated differently from one to which the library itself has decided to subscribe?
3. Which staff members have the authority to accept gifts.
4. How gifts will be processed, housed, accessed, etc. For example, is the library willing to set up special collections, collections that do not circulate, collections outside the library's collection development guidelines, etc.
5. The library's policy on appraisal. It is wise to state that the library only provides a letter listing the number of items donated.
6. The final disposition of materials not added to the collection (e.g., are they discarded, exchanged, or sold).

You may want to print the gift policy on a separate sheet to give to each patron who donates to the library.

COLLECTION MAINTENANCE

Weeding is a procedure not often included in policy statements. As a result, the public seldom understands what is kept, what is discarded, and why. It is important that the community understand this process and understand that it is a positive process. It is easy for people to get the wrong impression about weeding and feel that the library is discarding important materials.

Some key points to include in a weeding policy are the following:

1. What kind of material the library keeps—only current materials, a retrospective selection, or an in-depth collection. This can be a general statement and later defined on a subject by subject basis.
2. How the library deals with materials in areas which date rapidly, such as medicine, statistical compendiums, and the sciences.
3. Whether books listed in certain indexes, such as the *Essay and General Literature Index* will always be kept.
4. Whether the library discards previous editions of a book when a new edition is purchased.
5. Whether the number of circulations of a book is a criteria for discarding it, i.e., will the library discard a classic if it seldom circulates?
6. How the library deals with duplicates bought when the book was very popular but now hardly read. Does it put a title in deposit collections, give it to a local institution, sell it?
7. How the library deals with books in poor condition.
8. How the library handles selection mistakes.
9. How the library handles unused volumes which are part of a set of books.
10. How the library deals with books in subject areas no longer popular.

The following are some standard guidelines for weeding by subject which most policies do not include, since they have only tradition and experience rather than solid statistical or survey research behind them. You can find equally good ones in many textbooks on weeding.

Reference. Weed by subject, replace encyclopedias at least once every five years (more often if possible), replace yearbooks, statistical guides, and almanacs annually.

Religion, Philosophy, and Psychology. Keep basic information on religions and philosophy and the work of major writers. Discard secondary information based on use or which deal with subjects no longer of interest to the community. Keep a basic collection of books on standard psychological theories and the work of major writers. Discard self-help psychology books which are no longer popular.

Social Sciences, Education, and Folklore. Weed frequently—particularly economics books, which date quickly. Keep historical works but weed contemporary works which have been updated. Weed education materials in areas where techniques and ideas have changed. Keep basic material in folklore.

Language. Keep dictionaries, replace old grammars. Weed based on use.

Pure Science. Replace at least every three to five years except botany and natural history, which have a longer life. Pick up new trends in the sciences by reading reviews in specialized periodicals.

Applied Science, Health, Medicine, Cooking, Gardening, Business. Much of this area dates rapidly. Much of the applied science material, health, and medicine may be out of date in less than five years. However, older appliance and equipment manuals may be of use to community residents. Weed cookbooks and gardening books since a fresh new section is much more appealing. Keep current works on business and weed older ones based on use. Be particularly careful in the areas of finance, investment, and taxation.

Art, Music, and Hobbies. Weed based on use. Older material is valuable in these subject areas.

Literature. Keep plays, poetry, etc., unless they were written by little-known writers no longer read. Discard literary history which has been updated and works about minor writers.

History and Travel. Keep the classics on various periods of history, discard memoirs and personal accounts no longer read, discard personal travel accounts if dated and unread and older editions of guidebooks.

Biography. Weed biographies of people no longer of interest.

Fiction. Use standard lists as a basis for weeding. Discard duplicate copies of best-sellers no longer being read.

Subjects in Nonbook Formats. Special guidelines are needed for periodicals, pamphlets, audiovisual materials, and any other materials that the library acquires. These are harder to determine since they often require that the selector view or listen to the item in order to judge. It is harder to browse an audiocassette than a book. Library staff often rely on patron feedback to indicate physical troubles. It is a good idea to try to write some weeding guidelines particularly for audiovisual materials so that everyone is aware of the need to weed them. For example, a weeding policy for videos might include:

1. The information on the video is out-of-date.
2. The video is no longer of interest to the community as indicated by lack of use.
3. The video has been damaged.

EVALUATION AND INVENTORY

How will you evaluate the collection and at what intervals? Will you base the evaluation on your own judgment, on usage, by checking basic bibliographic tools, or a combination of all? Inventory, which impacts on the evaluation and decisions about replacements, should also be mentioned.

A section on evaluation and inventory is very rare in collection development policies. Although inventory procedures are valuable to know since they result in an evaluation of the current collection, the process is usually developed slowly over the history of the library. If these procedures exist, they are usually in a procedural document, which sometimes accompanies the policy document. That way, if the policy is updated by the board of directors, the procedures do not have to go through the same process. There are some published inventory procedures which, if your library does not have such a document, might help you create one. In the case of procedures, the development process is far less time consuming and financially burdensome than that of the collection development plan. One person can usually do it, with others editing and correcting it. That is far less labor intensive than the process being presented in this book for the policy side of collection development.

SPECIAL COLLECTIONS

If your library has a special collection with different selection, weeding, and other policy criteria, the collection development policy has to cover it separately. Most small and medium-sized libraries have few special collections, but many have a local history collection. Guidelines for a local history collection might include the following:

1. The kinds of materials the library collects—only books or books, letters, papers, documents, and maps.
2. Whether both primary and secondary source materials are collected.
3. Whether the library shares the collecting responsibility with a town agency or a historical society.
4. Whether local genealogical records are included.
5. Where materials appropriate to the collection can be donated.

NETWORKS

Since most small libraries cannot meet all the needs of their patrons, they no doubt belong to a network which gives them access to the collections of larger libraries. This should be spelled out in the policy statement so library users know that they can request books not available locally or can use other libraries that are members of the same library system. You'll want to describe your library's relationship with the libraries of other educational institutions such as school media centers, the libraries of colleges and universities, and special libraries in the community or in nearby communities. Are there specific reciprocal lending agreements in effect? Can public library users go directly to these institutions?

INTELLECTUAL FREEDOM, CENSORSHIP, AND LEGAL ISSUES

It is important that your written policy clearly state that the library buys a wide variety of materials to meet the needs of its diverse population and to achieve as balanced a collection as possible—one representing different points of view. It should be understood that materials are not excluded from the collection because of an author's race, nationality, sex, or political, social, or religious views. You should also note that the library does not label materials and does not set up special closed-shelf collections. It should also be clear that what children read is the responsibility of their parents.

Since public libraries serve a diverse public, which will not always agree with the library's selection decisions, you should establish a complaint review procedure. Have a form for the patron who is bringing the complaint. It should explain the library's review procedure and ask the patron to identify and describe the offending material. There should be an internal mechanism for reviewing the material in question and responding to the patron. Some libraries have a small committee which studies reviews of the material, examines the material itself, and recommends how the complaint should be answered. It should be clear in the policy that all complaints are treated seriously by the library and that the user will receive a letter from the library director after the examination is completed. Appeal can be made to the board of trustees. Library users should be made aware of the American Library Association's Freedom to Read Statement and the Library Bill of Rights, which are the bases for all library collection development policies.

CONFIDENTIALITY OF RECORDS

The issue of confidentiality of library records has become such an acute problem in recent years that the collection development policy should have a statement about it. The American Library Association has a statement to which you can refer. It is important for your patrons to feel that they can borrow materials without their reading habits being revealed, unless appropriate legal documents are presented to the library.

The collection development policy contains most of the following sections:

- mission, goals, objectives
- community analysis
- materials selection
- maintenance
- evaluation
- special collections
- networks, consortiums, cooperation
- intellectual freedom, censorship, and the law.

GETTING THE LIBRARY'S POLICY ADOPTED

Once the collection development policy is written, it has to be officially adopted by the board of trustees. Board members will want to discuss the document carefully and be sure they completely understand it before approving it. The process of getting the policy approved by the board can be difficult and each library director deals with his or her board differently. It is important to have the policy adopted so that the board is not surprised if there are any complaints arising from the collection itself, or about items in the collection. The policy is only an official one after the governing body, the board of trustees, approves it. Although many librarians decide not to waste the time and effort that it may take to get board approval, it is worthwhile when the library is challenged on one of its policies. You should underscore the controversial side of intellectual freedom, confidentiality, and other legal issues that are policy matters—an unprepared board is as bad as one that has never approved the policy. Explain the process and the policy in detail, and then lobby to get it through. One of the reasons that the process described in this book stresses the inclusion of board members in the development of the policy is that there should already be a basic understanding of the collection development policy, and the adoption of the policy by the board should be a relatively straightforward process. After the new policy is approved, it should be forwarded to the appropriate town governing body so that it is aware of the existence of the policy and knows what it contains. Once adopted, every effort should be made to publicize it. Plan presentations at community meetings, as well as press releases announcing the document. Copies of the collection development policy should be made available to the community upon request. Consider publishing a condensed version. Carefully note comments and questions from the community so that they can be dealt with in future revisions.

REFERENCES

Collection Development Plan for the Skokie Public Library, written and compiled by Merle Jacob, Coordinator of Collection Development and the Adult and Youth Services Librarians of the Skokie Public Library. June 1990.

Futas, Elizabeth. *Library Acquisition Policies and Procedures*, 2nd edition. Phoenix, Ariz.: Oryx Press, 1984.

"Guidelines for the Formulation of Collection Development Policies." *Library Resources and Technical Services* 21 (Winter 1977): 40-47.

Jacob, Merle. "Get It In Writing: A Collection Development Plan for the Skokie Public Library." *Library Journal* (September 1, 1990): 166-169.

Moore, Carolyn. "Core Collection Development in a Medium-Sized Public Library." *Library Resources and Technical Services* 24 (January/March 1982): 37-46.

Norman, Ronald V. "A Method of Book Selection for a Small Public Library." *RQ* 7 (Winter 1977): 143-145.

Scholtz, James. *Developing and Maintaining Video Collections in Libraries.* Santa Barbara, Calif.: ABC-Clio, Inc., 1989.

Segal, Joseph R. *Evaluating and Weeding Collections in Small and Medium-Sized Public Libraries: The Crew Manual.* Chicago: American Library Association, 1980.

Slote, Stanley. *Weeding Library Collections—II*, 2nd revised edition. Littleton, Colo.: Libraries Unlimited, 1982.

6 SUMMARY

In order to develop a collection and a collection development policy, data must be gathered and representatives of the library and community must be consulted. This is not something that can be accomplished in a short period of time, or alone. The greatest need in formulating a collection development policy is for ideas—these ideas must come from different people and different points of view. Even the smallest library must gather ideas from a number of people interested in keeping the library alive, vital, and a part of the community it serves.

In the preceding chapters, an attempt has been made to show, in detail, the steps that need to be taken to determine the kind of collection that will be tailor-made for a specific library. In this final chapter, the authors will walk you through these steps in the order that they have been promulgated in the text. One caveat to the consumer is that the way in which this process has been presented is only one of many possible permutations and combinations of process and ideas for developing library collections and collection development policies. In some libraries it might be wise to start at a different point, and in some places to end at a different point. The libraries that the authors have dealt with have mainly started where this volume has. They have then gone on to policy formation and from there to the selection and building of a collection suitable for that particular library. The final step in the process we described has been the evaluation and then the weeding from the collection of materials that do not fit the community's requirements. Only the people who are interested in a community and its cultural resources really can know the best way to go about this development. In the end, it is only these people, and the professionals that guide them, who can determine the best way to design a library for a community.

In the previous chapters, the art and science of collection development has been explained in some detail. Examples have been used to highlight some of the points of the process of collection development. In this summary chapter, we would like to present to you, the reader, in outline form, the steps to take to begin the process of developing a collection for a *specific* library in a *particular* community. In presenting these steps here, it is hoped that the reader will go back into the text for complete explanations of the various choices and will find the examples presented in the text helpful as they develop collections for small and medium-sized libraries.

1. BEGIN

As easy as it is to write this word, that is how difficult many people find doing it. Do not be daunted by the preplanning and other financial, time, and energy commitments that must be made. Start by deciding to do so. After the initial commitment, the rest is just figuring out where to find the concomitant time, energy, and money. For some people, decision making is very difficult; for these people, the beginning is the worst time. Once the initial decision has been made, everything will follow from that point, even if it does not follow as smoothly as you want it to. Nothing ever does. Remember, the process that results in the product is just as important as the product itself, some even believe more important. Also remember, once the process has been completed, it should begin again.

2. INVOLVE PEOPLE

No matter how small or how large the library organization, a number of people, more than one or two should be involved in this process. From the beginning of the process, try to involve the people you will need to successfully complete it. Make sure that everyone who wants to be involved will be and everyone who has to be involved will want to be. Troublemakers in any organization present problems. The place for troublemakers in a group situation is in the front, where you can see what they are doing.

3. MEET

The third step is to come together as a group to discuss both the product and the process that is intended to be carried out. This is the meeting at which it is most important to outline the process and at which ideas are exchanged. It can be the most important meeting of all, because it is the one at which people jockey for positions within the group, take on their eventual group roles, and begin building true consensus. It is important that the facilitator at this meeting be good, since the process and product that finally evolve are probably due more to the dynamics of this meeting than any other. These first meetings, in which the agendas are not filled with reports from subcommittees, can be difficult because they are not easily controllable. It is easier to control meetings where the agenda is set than it is to control discussions of people with differing ideas. Yet it is just these differences of opinions, preferences, needs, and outlooks that are so important to the process. Arguments should be encouraged, and constructive criticism should be helped along. An atmosphere of critical support should be engendered so that all feel comfortable being criticized and criticizing others without causing hurt feelings, losing friends, or worrying about retaliation from supervisors.

4. ORGANIZE

Since there are a number of tasks to perform and a number of ideas to be discussed, an organizational meeting of the entire group should start soon after the process has begun. Further organization into smaller groups with specific assignments should follow shortly. It is at this point that the librarian must decide who will be used as part of the collection development group: professionals, support staff, trustees, friends, volunteers, etc. Within these smaller groups (or if the library is too small, the whole group), each member takes on certain responsibilities. Presentations of facts are made to the smaller groups on an informal, but frequent basis. The larger group should meet every month or so to get everyone working in conjunction with one another and to bring about a melding of functions.

5. LEAD THE GROUP

It is important that everyone begin to feel the importance of what they are doing so that each will try to achieve the goals of the group and begin to have a sense of common needs and common goals. When one achieves success, all will achieve success. The person who runs the process should either know something about conducting meetings and organizing groups for work or should learn about it. There are books, pamphlets, and consultants who can help the leader to learn how to handle people in groups to achieve the best possible processes, should it be necessary.

6. GATHER INFORMATION

There are two areas (both fully explained in chapters three and four) in which information must be gathered. One is the library and its collection and the other is the community, which the library serves. In collecting information about the library, you must not forget to collect information on circulation, selection, hours, staffing, budgets, statistics, and in-house usage, as well as about its collection. When gathering information about the community, do not only investigate the needs of patrons of the library but question others in the community who may not use the library.

At the first few group meetings discuss the way in which information will be sought, what will be expected, and the deadlines so that each person understands what and where responsibilities lie. Questionnaires and interview questions must be designed and pretested, as well as all the various agencies combed to find the statistical information that exists in the community. The gathering of information is the longest part of the process. No timeline can be determined for these two areas since a lot depends on how much information is being collected. It can take as short a period as a few weeks or as long as several months. Persevere. It is an important part of the process.

7. ANALYZE AND SYNTHESIZE

The information about the library, its patrons, and its collections, as well as the community as a whole must not only be gathered but analyzed and synthesized. It should then be put into a format so that decisions based on this data can be implemented. Making decisions about selection, maintenance, evaluation, and weeding are the end products of the gathering of all the information and its analysis and synthesis. Very often when data are collected, just the raw figures are looked at and no conclusions are drawn. This is the fate of many of the statistics kept by libraries (and other institutions, businesses, etc.) What is the use of information if it does not lead to something. Your job at this step is to see that the information collected has a purpose. After all, decision making is what it is all about. The best information will get you nowhere if the correct interpretation of it is not made. There are many methods of analysis, and having a good statistician around to look at the data collected, at least in the census and questionnaire parts of the information gathering, would be a good idea. It is valuable now to go over some of the statements that are part of the the library's traditional philosophy, goals, and mission, if they exist. If they do not exist currently, by the data-analysis stage they should be in draft form. Be sure to have them considered by the widest number of people involved in the process.

8. EVALUATE

How "good" is the collection you now have. The results of the analysis and synthesis can be used to determine the answers to this question. If you have no idea for whom the library is being run, or what exactly is in the library, how can you judge its quality. All subjective information must be made on good judgment based on good information. The criteria by which to judge the collection must be discussed along with the interests of the community. In the case of the collection development process, make decisions on: the value of the collection; how to select and weed the collection; what kind of materials, subjects, and formats the library should supply; and any kind of services the library might provide but does not currently.

9. DEVELOP A POLICY STATEMENT

When all the data are in and everything has been looked at and put in the right perspective for this particular library, it is time to develop a policy based on all that has been determined. All the parts of a policy are discussed in chapter five. Certainly not all libraries need all the parts of the policy in a written document, but most need, at the very least, the following:

- A needs assessment statement that marks out the boundaries of the community to be served.
- A description of the clientele that discusses who is to be served by the collection that is developed.
- A statement of the philosophy of service that includes the goals, objectives, mission, and priorities of the library in regard to its community and its patrons.
- A selection statement that includes criteria, principles, formats, subjects, and responsibilities.
- An evaluation procedure including the criteria for determining whether the collection is of value to patrons and the community. On what basis is the label "good" to be applied. This part of the written document might include a procedures manual that exactly sets out how to go about an evaluation of the collection.
- A statement regarding maintenance of the collection that includes replacement, mending, binding, duplication of titles or volumes, plus the weeding of the collection, and the procedures to be followed in doing so.
- An intellectual freedom statement concerning the overarching principle against censorship and how it is dealt with in this particular library. It is not enough to append statements such as the *Library Bill of Rights* or the *Freedom to Read Statement* to an already existing policy, which contains everything else. It is important to write your own statement about the library and what its librarians think about censorship. In some instances, usually where there have been censorship problems, a procedures manual is enclosed in, or appended to, the written collection development policy.
- A review statement concerning how long it will be before the process is repeated (usually three to five years).
- A formal passage of the policy statement through the governing body of the library (Board of Trustees of a public library or Board of Directors) is the final step. Without this step the foregoing policy and the process that led up to it are just interesting exercises for the people who participated in them.

FIGURE 6-1 CYCLICAL PROCESS OF COLLECTION DEVELOPMENT

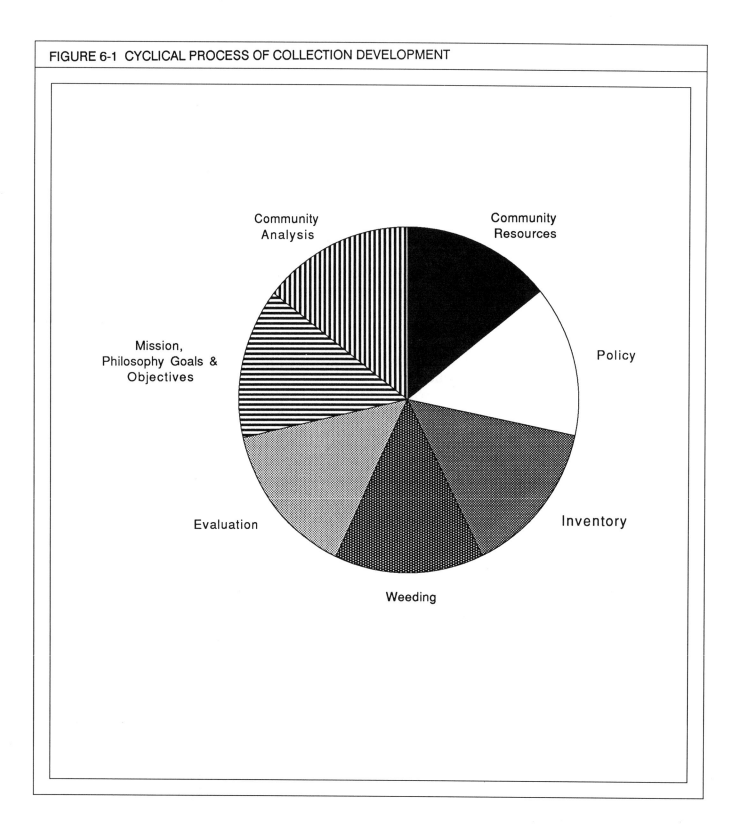

10. REITERATE

Now that the process has gone through one full cycle, do it over again! This time, correct any mistakes that were made. The full process, the very first time, is only finished with the second reiteration of the process. This chart, Figure 6-1, will serve to remind you of the most important steps.

Now that the product exists in a state that has passed the governing body, and the process has been completed, the library may decide to use the process, the product, and the individuals who participated in them to do library promotion with the community that the library serves. A good way to do that is to have the policy ready for distribution to the people who come into the library, to send it out to the voters, to go to country fairs, street fairs, or other "shows" to have a table set up for just the library and staffed by professionals and other individuals connected with the library to "talk-up" the library to the entire community. If there are well-attended town meetings, this might be an appropriate time to bring forth this public relations document. If you can get the community to talk about the library, it may give you more visibility in your community. Visibility is an important commodity for tax supported institutions. Do not let the community forget what the library is for. Try to get more people to use the library, its collections, and its materials. This is the way to a better collection!

A MODEL COLLECTION DEVELOPMENT POLICY

The library for which this policy was created does not exist except in the minds of the authors of this volume who have conjured it up.

BACKGROUND

The Futas-Cassell Memorial Free Public Library (FCMFPL) is located in a suburban community, Williamsville, of a medium-sized urban city, Gotham, and serves a population of 35,000 middle-class and working-class individuals. It is a growing community, with a strong Hispanic minority population and another growing minority of single-parent families, most of whom are headed by women. The income level is between $15,000 and $50,000 and in many family situations, both husband and wife work full-time. The majority of adults are high-school graduates and have some postsecondary education. There is a group of professionals who have college and postbaccalaureate degrees. A housing boom has brought a population shift from the city to its surrounding suburbs—Williamsville is one of them. Our town has three elementary schools, two middle schools, one high school, and a community college, which is part of the state's higher-education system. A number of shopping malls on the outskirts of town offer residents restaurants, good shopping, and movie complexes. There are four houses of worship in town which offer religious instruction, as well as social, service, and study groups.

The public library is legally run by a Board consisting of ten men and women appointed by the office of the mayor. They sit for a three-year term which can be renewed indefinitely. The library employs five full-time-equivalent librarians—a library director, a children's librarian, a technical services librarian, and the equivalent of two reference positions (a job shared by three part-time people.) The library is open 60 hours a week: Monday through Thursday 9:00 to 9:00 and Friday and Saturday 9:00 to 5:00. The collection comprises 60,000 books and 150 periodical subscriptions with 2,500 volumes in the reference collection, 3,500 volumes in the children's room, and 500 titles on records and tapes. The library circulates books, periodicals, audiotapes, videotapes, toys, puzzles, and art works. The circulation per year is 150,000. The library occupies 40,000 square feet and includes a room for library programs, film showings, storytelling programs, and for town meetings.

In a community survey done by the mayor's staff with input from the library staff, a great deal was learned about the town residents. Many residents spend their leisure time on projects centered around their homes: gardening, remodeling and redecorating, barbecuing, etc. They belong to a number of service and hobbyist organizations like the Lion's Club or Chess Club and participate in organized sports with their families.

POLICY

The following policy was written by the individuals most concerned with the library and presented to its Board of Trustees. It was passed a little over a year ago, and to date, nothing has been changed, although the year began with a review of the policy statement.

INTRODUCTION AND DESCRIPTION

Williamsville is an active and growing suburban community of 35,000 residents, the largest majority of whom work in Gotham, which is fifteen miles northwest. There is, and has been for the past five years, a population shift from the southeast sections of Gotham to this town. Since the population shift was expected, schools were built and the public library successfully passed a capital bond issue to build a 15,000 square foot addition onto the existing library.

STATEMENT OF PHILOSOPHY AND GOALS

Ideas are among the most powerful of human forces and knowledge a most essential tool for modern living. Since access to these ideas and this knowledge, through the written, audio, and visual media is so important, it is the philosophy of the Futas-Cassell Memorial Free Public Library to serve all the people of Williamsville equally and impartially to the best of its ability. Toward that end, the library seeks to purchase and retain the best and most useful material to fulfill its goals.

The goals of the FCMFPL are to:

1. meet the informational needs of the entire community,
2. assist individuals in achieving intellectual and spiritu-

al growth and to enjoy life to the fullest through recreational reading and viewing,

3. supplement formal study and encourage informal self-evaluation and learning,
4. stimulate thoughtful participation in the affairs of the community, the country, and the world by providing access to a variety of opinions on matters of current interest,
5. aid in learning and improving job-related skills.

OBJECTIVES

To meet the goals set forth in this policy statement, the following objectives have been adopted:

1. Serve the population of Williamsville by making information available to it in many formats for personal and private use.
2. Identify groups of people with specialized informational needs and purchase materials they will be able to use.
3. Act as a cultural and educational resource for the community by inviting lectures, demonstrations, and discussions to take place in the library building.
4. Enhance the acceptance of new technology for making lives easier and better by example and by expanding the collection of materials in those areas.

PURPOSE OF THE POLICY

The purpose of this policy statement is to clarify for the public and library staff the criteria used for selecting material, as well as the responsibility for the collection. We have included goals and objectives, as well as a description of the community and the philosophy of the library, to put these criteria into perspective.

SELECTION

The materials for our library must be selected with the purpose of carrying out the goals of this institution. To help in the process of selection, the following criteria are among those used to judge the quality and quantity of the items that are chosen:

The overarching criteria for the selection of any material are value, need, reception, format, and availability.

NONFICTION

1. Purpose and importance
2. Authority and reputation
3. Accuracy
4. Style, clarity, presentation
5. Access
6. Format
7. Need
8. Demand
9. Price
10. Relationship to other items in collection

FICTION

1. Style
2. Creativity, vitality
3. Characterization
4. Literary merit, significance
5. Appeal
6. Authenticity
7. Demand
8. Price
9. Need
10. Relationship to other items in collection

Individual titles used in selecting materials are listed in the appendix to this policy and are subject to additions, deletions, and changes. On occasion, reception may also refer to an item which is talked about, but which may not be reviewed, or may be reviewed negatively. Such an item may also belong on the shelves of the library to familiarize citizens with what is going on in the outside world.

RESPONSIBILITY FOR SELECTION

The responsibility for selecting material legally rests in the hands of the governing body of this library—the Board of Trustees. It, in turn, delegates this to the professional staff, which becomes responsible for the development of the collection on a day-to-day basis. In some areas, committees, individuals, or groups on the staff are more specifically delegated to select material; these responsibilities are listed in the part of this policy statement concerning selection.

There are numerous areas in which the Futas-Cassell Memorial Free Public Library has set up additional or alternative selection criteria, principles, and/or responsibilities.

[An example in each category is presented, with a partial list of other items within the category.]

CLIENTELE

The clientele of the library includes adult, young adult, and children, and may include adult independent learners; specific racial, ethnic, or religious groups within the community; physically disabled, institutionalized, retirees, etc.

Young Adults

Our library seeks to contribute to the understanding of the problems of development within this group especially as regards their physical, mental, and emotional well-being. The levels of competence and library skills vary greatly within this age group, and items are selected by the children's and reference librarians with an eye to these differences. The collection is fluid, flexible, current, and attractive and contains material mainly in paperback with an expected high turn-over rate. Important topics and favorite authors, as well as records, tapes, and videos, are selected specifically for this group. Young adults who seek out adult material will be encouraged; those who seek out juvenile material will also be helped. Although the goals of the institution stand also for this group, demand is seen as an important reason for inclusion. Specific criteria are:

- a wide range of subjects, some controversial;
- materials to encourage reading for pleasure and, therefore, set up a habit of life-long recreational reading;
- portrayal of young adults in an honest, nonsentimental, nonauthoritative way;
- recognition of special characteristics of this age group and the need to identify with others, peer pressure in the areas of behavior and conduct, and a search for self-identity, self-worth, and independence from family.

SUBJECTS

Certain subject areas may pose problems, notably religion, politics, medicine, and philosophy. There are also areas which are not necessarily controversial but which need carefully defined parameters because of the expense of the material or the restricted usefulness for the particular library such as art and genealogy.

RELIGION

The Williamsville library practices tolerance and attempts to present all of the world's religions through their own materials (e.g., Bibles) and enlightened material about them. In addition, the library attempts to select well-written books on comparative religions, Biblical interpretations, church history, religious education, and inspirational literature of all kinds. The collection is not large, but is kept up-to-date by conscientious weeding. Since there are courses taught in religious studies at the community college, and four active religious communities within the town, individuals with a greater need for in-depth materials are requested to borrow from another collection through interlibrary loan.

FORMATS

The library collects a number of formats especially in the area of audiovisual materials. Among these are films, records, audio cassettes, slides, and pictures. Other formats which are also part of a modern library's collection include paperbacks, periodicals, newspapers, pamphlets, textbooks, maps, and microforms. Newer formats such as videotapes, computer software, and compact disks are being added as funding allows. The latest that we have developed criteria for is videotapes.

Videotapes

It has been a policy of this library to purchase film in favor of video and to purchase instructional and educational videos in 3/4-inch format. The overwhelming acceptance of the 1/2-inch video format for all kinds of films, and the knowledge that there is a demand for this material, has made itself felt within the library in the past few years. The responsibility for selecting this material rests with a committee of librarians (three reference people and the children's librarian) using criteria similar to those of our book collection. Additional criteria include:

1. Material more appropriate in print form will not be purchased in video, just for the sake of the format.

2. A balanced collection of entertainment, documentary, instruction, and cultural material will be purchased.
3. Particular attention will be paid to a classic collection of children's videos that should last for several generations.
4. Since not all of the members of the community have equipment on which to play videos, two VHS videocassette recorders will be purchased to be borrowed with the videos.
5. A small percentage of the book budget (10 percent) will be used to extend this collection each year, and the staff will be encouraged to seek foundation and outside funding sources to build a worthwhile collection more rapidly. When the collection is built, the library will go to the town to ask for additional funding to keep the collection up-to-date.

MISCELLANEOUS
This section includes information on: rental collections, art, government publications, gifts, and toys.

Gifts
The Futas-Cassell Memorial Free Public Library of Williamsville encourages gifts of material or money for material by groups or individuals, citizens of the town or beyond, foundations, corporations, etc. These gifts must meet standard criteria; any materials received will be discarded if the library cannot use them. They will be offered to hospitals and jails in the state.

The library actively seeks bequests and memorials to honor those in the community who have been faithful patrons and supporters of the library and has memorial bookplates which can be attached to materials purchased with money donated for this purpose. Groups or collections of materials cannot necessarily be kept together as a group, and the library will most likely not be able to accept such gifts because of the financial costs of handling them. The library cannot be responsible for the appraisal of gifts for income tax or any other purposes.

LEVELS OF COLLECTION
Academic libraries have been using levels of collection develop-

ment for some time; it might be wise for public libraries to do the same. As a small library, however, we should not seek to use the levels defined for an academic institution. Comprehensive and research levels are used only by the largest public libraries which serve a research function in their cities, such as Boston Public Library, Chicago Public Library, and Providence Public Library. For libraries like the FCMFPL, the remaining levels should be redefined in the policy statement as follows:

Recreational Level: The best current titles on the subject which would include a well-selected group. Some, especially those without individual value over time, might be rented and not added to the collection at all.

General Information Level: A large number of current titles and a limited number of retrospective titles on any subject which would include those beyond the best-seller list. Only duplicate copies of the most asked for would be rented from this level. Others would be purchased, added to the collection, and retained over time.

Instructional Level: A good selection of current titles and a selection of retrospective titles. This would include some retrospective purchasing in new fields that reach this level, and a careful perusal of physical condition for replacement, if necessary. Some duplication might be necessary and careful weeding based on circulation level should be done at the time of evaluation.

Reference Level: Most current titles and a wide assortment of retrospective titles. During evaluation, note should be taken not only of circulation figures but of other means of use, e.g., in-house by patrons and by the professional staff.

In addition to the levels of collection, the library also seeks to include a core of essential materials in all subjects, which would be necessary to meet the demands and goals of the community.

COLLECTION MAINTENANCE

The collection of this library is maintained through judicious weeding of outdated, outmoded, and worn out materials. If needed, these are replaced, rebound, or duplicated when purchased. An inventory of items is performed once a year to keep the collection usable. Weeding the collection is considered of primary value to the maintenance of a good collection. Book sales and distribution of weeded materials are done on a twice-yearly basis. Books donated to the library may be sold or given away at this time.

COLLECTION EVALUATION

During the yearly inventory, and as a guide to selecting quality material, certain lists are checked to determine whether the library has purchased books of a lasting nature for its collection. At this time ALA's *Notable Books*, *Notable Young Adult Books*, and *Notable Children's Books*, along with other lists, are checked. Any items missing from the collection found on these lists are purchased if possible. Procedures for evaluating materials are in our procedures manual which includes the forms used to determine the value of the individual items in the collection.

INTELLECTUAL FREEDOM AND CENSORSHIP

It is the policy of this library to purchase material based on the criteria presented above. A number of books and other material purchased that will meet these criteria may be offensive to certain members of the community. The library sees its function as a purveyor of information on many topics, levels, and opinions. To meet its goals and objectives, this library must protect the freedom of all to choose their own information in the style in which it is presented. To that end, we subscribe wholeheartedly to the "Library Bill of Rights" and its several interpretations, "The Freedom to Read Statement" and "The Freedom to View Statement," all of which are appended to this document.

The library is a unique institution and is charged with being an unbiased repository of recorded expression. To that end, any attempt by a group or individual to remove items from the collection, or to add items not meeting standards set by this policy, shall be fought by the staff, librarians, and the Board. Procedures for reconsideration of material are in the procedures manual, along with the forms used to fill out complaints. The Board has the legal responsibility for the collection and its protection under the First Amendment of the Bill of Rights of the United States Constitution.

CONSORTIUM, COOPERATIVES, AND NETWORKS

The Futas-Cassell Memorial Free Public Library hopes to be tied together in the future with a number of public libraries in this area through an automated circulation and cataloging system. This will mean a larger selection of materials for our patrons to use, but will also mean a larger call on the material here by others from the libraries in the consortium. The value of automation and the broadening of the library's collection far exceeds the use of our material by others.

In addition to official consortium agreements, the FCMFPL participates in a state-wide interlibrary loan network through the state agency. This is a multitype library network and we have the advantage of being able to borrow needed material.

REVIEW OF COLLECTION DEVELOPMENT POLICY

This policy shall be reviewed at the first meeting of the Board of Trustees every year. If there are sections requiring revision, they shall be reviewed by the staff and presented to the Board for its acceptance into this policy at that time.

B MATERIALS SELECTION AIDS

CURRENT: GENERAL

Belles Lettres: A Review of Books by Women. Box 987, Arlington, VA 22216. 6/yr.

Reviews literature by women in all genres.

Bloomsbury Review. Box 8928, Denver, CO 80201. 10/yr.

A magazine about books: reviews, previews and listings.

The Booklist. American Library Association, 50 E. Huron St., Chicago, IL 60611. Bimonthly except July and August.

Reviews adult, young adult, and children's materials—print and nonprint including films, video, filmstrips, and software. All titles reviewed are recommended for purchase. The "Reference Books Bulletin" section reviews reference books.

Bulletin of the Center for Children's Books. University of Chicago Press, Journals Division, Box 37005, Chicago, IL 60637. Monthly except August.

Reviews of children's and some young adult books include grade-level recommendations.

Choice. 100 Riverview Center, Middleton, CT 06457. 11/yr.

Although mainly for academic libraries, it reviews many titles not found in other standard review media. Special bibliographic essays are included as well as a regular section on periodicals. Nonprint materials are also reviewed.

Collection Building. Neal-Schuman Publishers, 23 Leonard St., New York, NY 10013. Quarterly.

Articles on issues related to collection development and columns of interest to those doing book selection.

Horn Book Magazine. Park Square Building, 31 St. James Ave., Boston, MA 02116. 6/yr.

Reviews of children's books and audiovisual materials from preschool to junior high school.

Kirkus Reviews. Kirkus Service, Inc., 200 Park Ave.S., New York, NY 10003. Semi-monthly.

A pre-publication book review source primarily of use to public and school libraries.

Library Journal. R. R. Bowker, 249 W. 17 St., New York, NY 10011. Semi-monthly (monthly in January, July, August, December).

Reviews adult books and audiovisual materials. Also publishes a number of special lists during the year—the best new reference books, the best new business books, etc.

New York Review of Books. 250 W. 57 St., New York, NY 10017. 22 /yr.

An intellectual's review of books. The reviews, by well-known writers, are lengthy bibliographical essays which deal with the subject as well as the book being reviewed.

New York Times Book Review. New York Times, 229 W. 43 St., New York, NY 10036. Weekly.

The weekly section of the Sunday *New York Times.* Reviews mostly adult books and a few children's books; occasional special sections on business books, children's books, etc. If available, try the Sunday book sections of the *Los Angeles Times* and the *Washington Post.*

Parnassus. 41 Union Square W., Rm. 804, New York, NY 10003. 2/yr.

In-depth analysis of contemporary books of poetry.

Previews; Professional and Reference Literature Review. Mountainside Publishers, Inc., 321 S. Main Street, #300, Ann Arbor, MI 48104. Monthly.

Summarizes reviews of reference materials from other sources citing where the review appeared and who reviewed it.

Publishers Weekly. R.R. Bowker, 249 W. 17 St., New York, NY 10011. Weekly.

A publication for the book trade, reviews a selected number of pre-publication fiction and nonfiction titles with special issues for children's books, religious books, etc. There is also a new section: "Audio/Video Plus," which reviews audio and video cassettes.

Reference Service Review. Pierian Press, Box 1808, Ann Arbor, MI 48106. Quarterly.

A publication devoted to reviewing reference materials; includes bibliographic articles as well.

RQ. American Library Association, 50 E. Huron St., Chicago, IL 60611. Quarterly.

The official publication of the Reference and Adult Service Division, *RQ* reviews reference books as well as publishing articles on various aspects of reference service.

San Francisco Review of Books. 117 Geary St., San Francisco, CA 94109. 6/yr.

A literary review focusing on non-best-sellers.

School Library Journal. R.R. Bowker, 249 W. 17 St., New York, NY 10011. Monthly except June and July.

Includes reviews of children's and young adult books and audiovisual materials.

Science Books and Films; The Quarterly Review. American Association for the Advancement of Science, 1776 Massachusetts Avenue N.W., Washington, DC 20036. Quarterly.

A review of books and nonprint materials on the pure and applied sciences for students of all levels and the general public.

Small Press. Meckler Publishing, 11 Ferry Lane W., Westport, CT 06880. Bimonthly.

Reviews of small-press books as well as articles on the small-press world.

Vertical File Index. H. W. Wilson, 950 University Ave., Bronx, NY 10452. Monthly.

A listing of inexpensive, paperbound materials.

VLS (Voice Literary Supplement.) Village Voice, 842 Broadway, New York, NY 10003. Monthly.

A monthly supplement of the *Village Voice* with reviews of

current books. It often features bibliographic essays on the works of contemporary writers.

Voice of Youth Advocates. Scarecrow Press, 52 Liberty St., Box 4167, Metuchen, NJ 08840. Bimonthly.

Reviews print and nonprint materials for young adults as well as professional materials. Articles on young adult services.

Wilson Library Bulletin. H. W. Wilson, 950 University Ave., Bronx, NY 10452. Monthly except July and August.

Columns with reviews: "Current Reference Books," "On Record," and a "Software for Libraries." Sometimes provides bibliographic essays.

Women's Review of Books. Wellesley College Center for Research on Women, Wellesley, MA 02181. Monthly.

In-depth reviews of books by and about women in all areas.

Retrospective

American Reference Books Annual (ARBA). Littleton, Co: Libraries Unlimited.

Reviews reference books annually.

Children's Catalog. Bronx, N Y: H. W. Wilson, 1986. 15th ed. Annual supplements.

A recommended list of the best fiction and nonfiction books for children—preschool to the sixth grade.

Fiction Catalog. New York: H. W. Wilson, 1991. 12th ed.

A recommended list of fiction titles for public and college libraries.

Lang, Jovian and Masters, Deborah, eds. *Reference Books for Small and Medium Size Libraries.* Chicago: American Library Association, 1984.

The title describes it well. A good place to begin for developing a reference collection in a smaller library.

Public Library Catalog. Bronx, N Y: H. W. Wilson Co., 1989. 9th ed. Annual supplements.

A recommended list of nonfiction titles for public libraries.

Reader's Adviser. 13th ed. New York: R.R. Bowker, 1986-88.

A six-volume set of which the first three have been published. It is a guide to the best of world literature, social sciences, history, arts, philosophy, religion, science, technology, and medicine.

Reader's Catalog; An Annotated Selection of More Than 40,000 of the Best Books in Print in 208 Categories, edited by Geoffrey O'Brien, et al. 250 W. 57th Street, New York, NY 10107. 1989.

The title tells all—a new guide to the best books in print. It is arranged by subject.

SERIALS

Katz, Bill and Katz, Linda Sternberg. *Magazines for Libraries.* 6th ed. New York: R. R. Bowker, 1989.

Recommendations on 6,500 periodicals arranged by subjects. This is supplemented by Katz's column in *Library Journal.*

RECORDINGS, COMPACT DISCS, AND AUDIOCASSETTES

American Record Guide. Washington, D. C.: Heldref Publications. 6/yr.

Focuses on reviews of classical recordings.

Audio Magazine. Box 5316, Boulder, CO 80302. Monthly.

Good music reviews on all styles of music. Sound and performances are evaluated.

CD Review. Box 58835, Boulder, CO 80322-8835. Monthly.

Includes CD reviews by category—classical, jazz, pop/rock, new age, country/folk, and stage/screen.

Down Beat. Maher Publications, 180 W. Park Ave., Elmhurst, IL 60126. Monthly.

Current record reviews of all kinds of popular music.

Fanfare. Box 720, Tenafly, NJ 07670. 6/yr.

A review medium for the serious record collector. Reviewers discuss the performance, the music, and the quality of the recording.

High Fidelity. ABC Consumer Magazines, 825 Seventh Ave., New York, NY 10019. Monthly.

Reviews of all kinds of records in all formats with special emphasis on classical records. Articles on music and equipment.

Rolling Stone. Box 55329, Boulder, CO 80322. Biweekly.

Reviews of popular music, especially rock.

Stereo Review. Box 2771, Boulder, CO 80302. Monthly.

Reviews of all kinds of records—both tape and disk—as well as music videos. Articles on video equipment.

Retrospective

The New Penguin Guide to Compact Discs and Cassettes. London: Penguin, 1988.

An evaluative guide to classical music with an annual update.

On Cassette, A Comprehensive Bibliography of Spoken-Word Audio Cassettes. New York: R. R. Bowker, 1985.

An extensive list of spoken-word cassettes with title, author, subject, and performer indexes.

FILMS AND VIDEO

Afterimage: A Monthly Journal of Photography, Independent Film, Video and Video Books. Video Studies Workshop, 31 Prince St., Rochester, NY 14607. 9/yr.

Contains up-to-date information on independent and video art films as well as articles on video artists and collections.

AFVA Evaluations. American Film and Video Association, 920 Barnsdale Road, Suite 152, LaGrange Park, IL 60525.

Evaluations of American Film and Video Festival entries and

award winners. The evaluations are compiled from comments from the jurors.

American Film. Box 966, Farmingdale, NY 11737-9866. Monthly.

Short reviews of new releases on VHS and Beta and of new films.

Information Technology & Libraries. American Library Association, Library and Information Technology Association, 50 E. Huron St., Chicago, IL 60611. Quarterly.

Under "Recent Publications," this periodical reviews videocassette programs of interest to libraries. This is the official publication of the Library and Information Technology Association.

New York Times. Sunday edition. Arts & Leisure Section.

"Home Video" column contains information on VCRs for home use and reviews of entertainment videos.

Sightlines. American Film and Video Association, 920 Barnsdale Road, Suite 152, LaGrange Park, IL 60525. Bimonthly.

Reviews 16mm films and video releases.

Video. Box 56293, Boulder, CO 80322-6293. Monthly.

Columns of reviews of home video, music and narrative film entertainment titles are contained in "Programming." Laserdiscs are also reviewed. Articles on current technology and equipment.

Video Librarian. Box 2725, Bremerton, WA 98310. Monthly.

Articles on trends, equipment, and related topics as well as video reviews.

Video Review. Box 57751, Boulder, CO 80322-7751. Monthly.

Contains reviews of new feature films, music, and game videos as well as articles and reviews of technology and equipment.

Video Times. Publications International, 5615 W. Cermack Rd., Cicero, IL 60650. Monthly.

Reviews the video-cassette releases of feature films with an emphasis on classic and mass-market nontheatrical titles.

Retrospective

Halliwell's Film and Video Guide. 6th ed. New York: Scribner, 1987.

Lists approximately 10,000 titles. It is evaluative and does not attempt to describe the entire plot. Uses a star rating system to evaluate the titles listed.

Leonard Maltin's TV Movies and Video Guide. New York: New American Library, 1990.

An annual publication which lists about 17,000 titles with evaluative comments and a star rating system.

Limbacher, J. L. *Feature Films. A Directory of Feature Films on 16MM and Video Tape.* 8th edition. New York: R. R. Bowker, 1985.

Information on over 35,000 titles. Primarily educational titles. Not a review media.

Mason, Sally and Scholtz, James. *Video for Libraries; Special Interest Video for Small and Medium-Sized Libraries.* Chicago: ALA, 1988.

An annotated list of educational and informational videos as well as a core collection of feature films by James L. Limbacher.

Orlin, Leslie, ed. *Media Review Digest: The Only Complete Guide to Reviews of Non-Book Media.* Ann Arbor: Pierian Press. Annual.

A comprehensive list of reviews for all media formats in over 200 periodicals; 16 mm films, feature films, videotapes, filmstrips, etc. are included in Part I and spoken word record and tapes in Part II.

Scholtz, James. *Developing and Maintaining Video Collections in Libraries.* Santa Barbara, CA: ABC-Clio, Inc., 1989.

An excellent resource on all aspects of collecting videos.

Video Source Book. Detroit, MI: Gale Research, 1990.

A listing of over 40,000 programs currently available on video with a subject index. It includes both videotapes and disks.

BIBLIOGRAPHY

Armstrong, Patricia. "Automated Circulation: For the Small Public Library" *Canadian Library Journal* XLI (December 1984): 334-337.

Beckerman, Edwin P. "Administrator's Viewpoint; Collection Development in an Urban Setting: A Case Study and Responses" *Collection Building* V (Winter, 1984): 35-44.

Bertcher, Harvey J. and Maple, Frank R. *Creating Groups*. Beverly Hills, Calif.: Sage, 1977.

Bob, Murray L. "The Case of Quality Book Selection" *Library Journal* CVII (January 15, 1982): 1707-10.

————. "Library Use, Reading, and the Economy" *Library Journal* CX (February 15, 1985): 195-207.

Bone, Larry Earl, ed. "Community Analysis and Libraries" *Library Trends*, XXIV (January, 1976): 429-643.

Bonn, George S. "Evaluation of the Collection" *Library Trends* XXII (January, 1974): 265-304.

Bradford, Leland P. *Making Meetings Work: A Guide for Leaders and Group Members*. San Diego, CA: University Associates, 1976.

Broadus, Robert N. *Selecting Materials for Libraries*. 2nd ed. New York: H.W. Wilson, 1981.

Burdick, Amrita J. "Library Photocopying: The Margin of Caring" *The New Library Scene* 5 (June 1986): 17-18.

Callahan, Joseph A. *Communicating—How to Organize Meetings and Presentations*. New York: Franklin Watts, 1984.

Carpenter, Ray L. "The Public Library Patron" *Library Journal* CIV (February 1, 1979): 348.

Cassell, Kay Ann. *Knowing Your Community and Its Needs*. (Small Libraries Publications No. 14). Chicago: American Library Association, 1988.

Chatman, Elfreda A. "Low Income and Leisure: Implications for Public Library Use" *Public Libraries* XXIV (Spring 1985): 34-36.

Christiansen, Dorothy E., Davis, C. Roger, and Reed-Scott, Jutta. "Guide to Collection Evaluation Through Use and User Studies" *Library Resources & Technical Services* (October/December, 1983): 432-40.

Collection Development in Libraries: A Treatise. Edited by Robert D. Stueart and George B. Miller, Jr. Greenwich, Conn.: JAI Press, 1980.

Collister, Edward A. *The Preservation and Restoration of Library Materials: A Basic and Practical Reading List.* Monticello, Ill: Vance Bibliographies, 1985.

Comer, Cynthia. "List-checking As a Method for Evaluating Library Collections" *Collection Building* III (1981): 26-34.

Curley, Arthur and Broderick, Dorothy. *Building Library Collections.* 6th ed. Metuchen, N.J: Scarecrow Press, 1985.

Daniel, Wayne W. *Questionnaire Design: A Selected Bibliography for the Survey Researcher.* Monticello, Ill: Vance, 1979.

D'Elia, George, and Walsh, Sandra. "Patrons' Use and Evaluations of Library Services: A Comparison Across Five Public Libraries" *Library and Information Science Research* VII (January 1985): 3-30.

Evans, C. Edward. *Developing Library and Information Center Collections.* 2nd ed. Littleton, Colo.: Libraries Unlimited, Inc., 1987.

Fussler, Herman, and Simon, Julian Lincoln. *Patterns in the Use of Books in Large Research Libraries.* Chicago: University of Chicago Library, 1961.

Futas, Elizabeth, and Intner, Sheila S. "Collection Evaluation" issue of *Library Trends* (Winter, 1985): 237-436.

———. *Library Acquisition Policies and Procedures.* 2nd ed. Phoenix: Oryx Press, 1984.

———. *Library Acquisition Policies and Procedures.* Phoenix: Oryx Press, 1977.

———. *Library Forms Illustrated Handbook.* New York: Neal-Schuman, 1984.

Gardner, R. K. *Library Collections: Their Origins, Selection and Development.* New York: McGraw-Hill, 1981.

Goldhor, Herbert. "Community Analysis for the Public Library" *Illinois Libraries* LXII (April, 1980): 296-302.

———. "Some Measure of Adult Use of Public Library Books" *Illinois Libraries* LXII (October 1980): 641-643.

Greenfield, Jane. *Books: Their Care and Repair.* Bronx, NY: H.W. Wilson, 1984.

"Guidelines for the Formulation of Collection Development Policies," *Library Resources and Technical Services* XXI (Winter, 1977): 40-47.

Gunner, Jean. *Simple Repair and Preservation Techniques for Collection Curators, Librarians and Archivists.* 3rd ed. Pittsburgh: Hunt Institute for Botanical Documentation, 1984.

Henderson, Kathryn Luther, and Henderson, William T. *Conserving and Preserving Library Materials.* Champaign, Ill: University of Illinois, Graduate School of Library and Information Science, 1983.

Horton, Carolyn. *Cleaning and Preserving Bindings and Related Materials.* 2nd ed. Revised. Chicago: American Library Association, Library Technology Reports, 1969.

Hyman, Ronald T. *Improving Discussion Leadership.* New York: Columbia University Teachers College Press, 1980.

James, Stephen E. "The Relationship Between Local Economic Conditions and the Use of Public Libraries" *Library Quarterly* LV (July 1985): 255-272.

Johnson, David W., and Johnson, Frank P. *Joining Together: Group Theory and Group Skills.* Englewood Cliffs, N.J: Prentice-Hall, 1975.

Katz, William A. *Collection Development; The Selection of Materials for Libraries.* New York: Holt, Rinehart & Winston, 1980.

Kent, Allen, et al. *Use of Library Materials: the University of Pittsburgh Study.* New York: Marcel Dekker, 1979.

Kohl, Davis. *Circulation, Interlibrary Loan, Patron Use, and Collection Maintenance: A Handbook for Library Managers.* Santa Barbara, Calif.: ABC Clio, 1986.

Knowles, Malcolm and Knowles, Hulda. *Introduction to Group Dynamics.* Revised ed. Chicago: Associate Press, 1977.

Kronus, Carol L. "Patterns of Adult Library Use: A Regression and Path Analysis" *Adult Education* XXIII (Winter 1973): 115-131.

Kruger, Karen. *Coordinated Cooperative Collection Development for Illinois Libraries!* Springfield, Ill.: Illinois State Library, 1983. [Three volumes]

Kyle, Heidi, et al. *Library Materials Preservation Manual: Practical Methods for Preserving Books, Pamphlets and Other Printed Materials.* Bronxville, N.Y.: Nicholas T. Smith, 1983. (Published for the New York Botanical Gardens.)

Line, Maurice. *Library Surveys: An Introduction to Their Use, Planning,*

Procedure and Presentation. 2nd Ed. Revised by Sue Stone. London: Bingley, 1982.

Lucas, Linda. "Life Style, Reading, and Library Use" *Public Libraries* XVIII (Spring 1979): 22.

Martin, Allie Beth. "Studying the Community: An Overview" *Library Trends* XXIV (January 1976): 483-496.

Milevski, Robert J. "Book Repair Manual" *Illinois Libraries* 67 (October 1985): 648-684.

Monroe, Margaret E. "Community Development As a Mode of Community Analysis" *Library Trends* XXIV (January, 1976): 497-514.

Moore, Carolyn. "Core Collection Development in a Medium-Sized Public Library" *Library Resources and Technical Services* XXVI (January/March, 1982): 37-46.

Moran, Barbara B. "Construction of the Questionnaire in Survey Research" *Public Libraries* 24 (Summer 1985): 75-76.

Norman, Ronald V. "A Method of Book Selection for a Small Public Library" *RQ* XVII (Winter 1977): 143-5.

Osborn, Charles B. "Non-use and User Studies in Collection Development" *Collection Management* IV (Spring-Summer, 1982): 45-53.

Oppenheim, Abraham Naftali. *Questionnaire Design and Attitude Measurement.* New York: Basic Books, 1966.

Output Measures for Public Libraries; A Manual of Standardized Procedures. 2nd ed. Prepared for the Public Library Development Project by Nancy A. Van House, et al. Chicago: American Library Association, 1987.

Palmer, Barbara C., and Palmer, Kenneth R. *The Successful Meeting.* Englewood Cliffs, N.J.: Prentice-Hall, 1983.

Parker, Edwin B. and Paisley, William J. "Predicting Library Circulation from Community Characteristics" *Public Opinion Quarterly* XXXIII (Spring 1965): 39-53.

Payne, Stanley L. *The Art of Asking Questions.* Princeton: Princeton University Press, 1951.

Planning & Role Setting for Public Libraries; A Manual of Options and

Procedures. Prepared for the Public Library Development Project by Charles R. McClure, et al. Chicago: American Library Association, 1987.

Preservation of Library Materials. Edited by Joyce R. Russell. Proceedings of a seminar sponsored by the Library Binding Institute and the Princeton-Trenton Chapter of the Special Libraries Association held at Rutgers University, July 20-21, 1979. New York: Special Libraries Association, 1980.

Robbins-Carter, Jane, ed. *Public Librarianship, A Reader*. Littleton, Co.: Libraries Unlimited, 1982.

Schindler-Rainman, Eva, and Lippitt, Ronald. *Taking Your Meeting Out of the Doldrums*. La Jolla, Calif.: University Associates, 1977.

Segal, Joseph P. *Evaluating and Weeding Collections in Small and Medium-Sized Public Libraries: The Crew Manual*. Chicago: American Library Association, 1980.

Serebnick, Judith, ed. *Collection Management in Public Libraries*. Chicago: American Library Association, 1986.

Slote, Stanley. *Weeding Library Collections-II*. 2nd revised ed. Littleton, Co.: Libraries Unlimited, 1982.

Soltys, Amy. "Planning and Implementing a Community Survey" *Canadian Library Journal* XLII (October, 1985): 245-249.

Stevenson, Gordon. "Popular Culture and the Public Library" *Advances in Librarianship*, edited by Melvin J. Voigt and Michael H. Harris. New York: Academic Press.

Tropman, John E. *Effective Meetings: Improving Group Decision-Making*. Beverly Hills, Calif.: Sage, 1980.

Van Orden, Phyllis, and Phillips, Edith B., eds. *Background Readings in Building Library Collections*. 2nd ed. Metuchen, N.J.: Scarecrow, 1979.

Warncke, Ruth. *Studying the Community*. Chicago: American Library Association, 1960.

Warren, Roland Leslie. *Studying Your Community*. New York: Russell Sage Foundation, 1955.

White, Brenda H., ed. "Collection Management for School Library Media Centers" *Collection Management* VII (Numbers 3/4): 171-215.

Wiemers, Eugene, Jr. *Materials Availability in Small Libraries: A Survey Handbook.* Occasional Papers No. 149. Urbana-Champaign: University of Illinois Graduate School of Library and Information Science, 1981.

Wilson, Pauline. *A Community Elite and the Public Library; the Uses of Information in Leadership.* Westport, Ct.: Greenwood Press, 1977.

Wood, Leonard. "The Gallup Survey: Library Use: An Irregular Habit" *Publishers Weekly* CCXXVIII (November 22, 1985): 20-21.

Zweizig, Douglas and Dervin, Brenda. "Public Library Use, Users, Uses: Advances in Knowledge of the Characteristics and Needs of the Adult Clientele of American Public Libraries" *Advances in Librarianship.* Edited by Melvin J. Voigt and Michael H. Harris. New York: Academic Press, 1977.

INDEX

Kay Ann Cassell is Associate Director for Programs and Services, The Branch Libraries, New York Public Library.

Elizabeth Futas is Director, University of Rhode Island, Graduate School of Library and Information Studies, Kingston.

Book design: Gloria Brown
Cover design: Gregory Apicella
Typography: Roberts/Churcher